THE
JEWISH-CHRISTIAN
ARGUMENT

The Jewish-Christian Argument *A HISTORY OF THEOLOGIES IN CONFLICT*

by Hans Joachim Schoeps

TRANSLATED BY DAVID E. GREEN

HOLT, RINEHART AND WINSTON

NEW YORK • CHICAGO • SAN FRANCISCO

In memory of my brother Konrad,
born in Berlin on April 3, 1914,
died in Hohenlychen on June 17, 1936

In memory of my parents

My father, *Sanitätsrat* Dr. med. Julius Schoeps,
born on January 5, 1864 in Neuenburg/Westpreussen,
died on December 27, 1942 at Theresienstadt

and my mother, Kaete Schoeps, *née* Frank,
born on February 17, 1886 in Brandenburg/Havel,
murdered at Auschwitz, June, 1944

FOREWORD TO
THE FIRST EDITION

THE history of the dialogue between Israel and the Church, in their argument with each other on behalf of the truth, has not yet been written. In this book, I have endeavored to depict in broad strokes the course of this theological discussion through almost nineteen centuries, and to sketch the problems which have repeatedly arisen. If the history of this polemic were more generally known than it is—what thoughts have already been thought and what themes have already been touched upon—many recent arguments and much debate which seems relevant would have been settled long ago. The purpose of this book, therefore, is to assist in bringing the witness of the centuries to the Judaeo-Christian dialogue of our own day. We shall study a history of theology, in order that the present day may once more clearly perceive that portion of *Heilsgeschichte* which strives for realization through the Judaeo-Christian encounter of the ages.

The question with which this book deals has concerned me since the early days of my youth, in the course of which the question, "Jew or Christian?" had already confronted me, through the person of an older friend who was studying Protestant theology. At that time, both of us wrestled with passion over every sentence of Christian doctrine. Prior to that time, I had had no knowledge of matters pertaining to Judaism. Only much later did I discover that our arguments reflected nothing other than the centuries-old struggle between the Jewish and Christian faiths, and were thus a properly conducted discussion. The "no" which I finally said was said with difficulty, and even today I feel in all its old strength the demand that I vindicate this "no" in spirit and in truth. But in this book I am not writing confessions; I am seeking only to present, in bare outline, the answers given by the centuries. Yet today I can state that the dogmatic answers of tradition have, to a large extent, become my own answers—and this is probably the only possible legitimation for a Jewish speaker. For this reason, the reader must not expect from the author intellectual originality, or anything similar. No originality can be found here beyond that present in the selection, ordering, and presentation of material taken from the sources. As a consequence of its rare appearance these days, there is, however, one individual trait of which the author is aware: he is always able to view historical problems theologically, as well as to constantly observe theological problems against the background of history.

It remains only to state, by way of introduction, that many contributions to this theme of which I am aware—and probably even more of which I am not aware—have been omitted, in order that the boundaries of this study, which confine it to a primarily informatory purpose, may not be too far transgressed. The basic goal was to bring to light the ways of dealing with these questions which have become normative for Jewish written tradition. Nevertheless, merely to mention them in this connection, and particularly to work out the Jewish attitude toward Pauline theology, may open up new territory for scientific investigation. The characteristics of the Jewish faith have always achieved expression in the process of differentiation from alien doctrine. I am well aware that behind this presentation, there are and will remain serious problems belonging to the realm of systematic Jewish theology. Perhaps it will be granted me to contribute to their solution later in life. My *Jüdischer Glaube in dieser Zeit* (Berlin, 1932) contains prolegomena; a few remarks on the subject of phenomenology of religion will be found in the last chapter of this work.

This little book is dedicated to the memory of my brother, who, while still young, was taken from this earth. He often asked what makes the Jew a Jew, and the Christian a Christian. In large measure, I have continued to owe him the answer—and, unhappily,

much more besides. Therefore, it is in his memory that I set forth
what questions have arisen in the course of centuries, and what
answers have been essayed.

Berlin, January 1, 1937

FOREWORD TO
THE SECOND EDITION

THIS book made its first appearance in 1937, behind closed doors, as it were, for the authorities at that time in power in Germany allowed its sale only in Jewish bookstores and to Jews. Then, when it was noticed that it was a "dangerous" book, it was prohibited completely. Because I believe that it says things of fundamental importance, and deals with materials which are as good as unknown, I am having the book republished now.

During the subsequent years, which I spent in exile, I have engaged in further work in this field. But I did not want to burden this presentation with all the scholarly material appearing in print, some of which is present in my large-scale work *Theologie und Geschichte des Judenchristentums,* some in my volume *Aus frühchristlicher Zeit* (both published by J. C. B. Mohr, Tübingen). For this reason, only a small portion of the original text has been altered and supplanted; there is, however, an entirely new chapter.

For the new edition, I have had to extend the dedication of this book. On December 27, 1942, my father died in the concentration camp Theresienstadt; and in June of 1944, my mother was gassed at Auschwitz. In view of this experience, I ask myself today whether the period of religious dialogue may not perhaps be past; whether, with these senseless exterminations, something quite different has begun. However the case may be, the questions discussed in this book will continue to exist and to be relevant until the end of the world.

Erlangen, January 1, 1949

FOREWORD TO
THE THIRD EDITION

I OWE a special debt of gratitude to the Ner-Tamid-Verlag, Frankfurt, for making this book, long out of print, once again available to a wider audience. The previous edition was published at the time of the currency reform by a small publishing house which soon vanished from the scene, so that this book did not reach the readers asking for a reliable orientation to the theological debate between Judaism and Christianity. Because of the spiritual confusion and obfuscation of all objective positions in the past decade, there is a great need for clarification.

There is still only a small circle of theologians who today realize that Judaism represents a revealed religion, with fully developed articles of faith. There are fewer still who recognize the real points of difference between Israel and the Church. This book attempts to use the controversies of nineteen centuries as a mirror to reflect the inner relationship of tension between Judaism and Christianity. The dominant theme of this controversy, begun by the Church Fathers and the Rabbis of the early Talmudic period, and coming down to Martin Buber and Franz Rosenzweig, undergoes a development from conflict between dogmas to dialogue between two faiths.

In the process of making our age aware of the witness of the centuries, fallen into obscurity, it is abundantly clear that Judaism is in no better position today than in earlier epochs of its history to assume any unique event to be the ultimate revelation of God. This provides at the outset the differentiation of the Jewish and Christian paths through secular history. But both are united in sharing a common perspective, directed toward the future, seeing that the full truth is yet to come. As is stated at the end of this book, it is in the ancient petition of the *Pater Noster,* "thy kingdom come," that both religions are inextricably linked.

For this new edition, the text itself has not been altered, but the notes have been extended and the bibliographical references supplemented. The whole was given a new title, while the former title was retained as subtitle. There has been appended a list of pertinent books dealing with this subject which have appeared since 1945, together with a list of abbreviations. The book has probably reached its final form. May it have a salutary effect!

Erlangen, January 1, 1961

CONTENTS

THE
JEWISH-CHRISTIAN
ARGUMENT

I

THE ABSOLUTE
IN RELIGIOUS HISTORY

Introductory Remarks

THERE is a basic question which, despite its threatening nature, every work on comparative history of religion must force itself to ask. This is ultimately a question about the *absolute* nature of every revelation, which—acknowledged by faith—opposes and withdraws from all comparative methods which attempt to relativize it. To Ernst Troeltsch goes the credit for pointing out to an age unaccustomed to dogmatic thought this apparently insoluble apriori, in his lecture of 1901, since become famous: *Die Absolutheit des Christentums und die Religionsgeschichte.* The difficulty involved in formulating this question was only brought into sharper relief by his own endeavors, as well as those of his predecessors (for example, the work of the nineteenth-century historical school, and the studies of Wilhelm Dilthey in intellectual and religious history, which crowned this work). In spite of the optimism of Dilthey and Troeltsch, and almost all the thinkers of that era, the question cannot be answered unconditionally on the basis of "historical significance" alone or the "unified context of all that lives."

The theological debate between Judaism and Christianity— the theme to be discussed here—cannot be dealt with at all without a prior expression of the investigator's point of view regarding the problem of the absolute in secular and religious history. Thus the author feels compelled to state at the outset that he would never have begun this work had he not held the belief that in the Holy Scriptures, both *Tanakh* (the first letter of the Hebrew words for Pentateuch, Prophets, and Writings form this traditional locution) and Gospel, God's word speaks out in pure reality, piercing through the words of men, ever and again reaching our ears. Since the author is of the Jewish faith, for him the question of the absolute in religious history has found the answer that for the Jew, God's word is heard solely and exclusively in the *Tanakh;* the revelation of God to Israel needs no supplement, increase, or fulfillment. Needless to say, the *Tanakh* is also God's word for the Christian, just as it was for Jesus Christ as an historical person. No church wishing to retain the name of Christian Church can dispense with hearing the Scriptures of the "Old Testament." But the history recounted by these documents tells of the covenant of God with *one* nation, the nation of Israel, which, in full physical reality, goes through history ever since that occasion of grace as a covenant community, completely distinct from other nations. This history, with all its glories, trials, and punishments, has for the Church a sacred meaning such as can be found nowhere else in the world; but it is not the history of the Christian Church, which embraces all nations. For this reason the verdict from within Judaism must agree with that of Paul: to this day the veil of Moses hangs over the understanding of the Old Testament. (II Cor. 3:13,14)

What the Church proclaims as its essential mystery, revealed as truth to the Christian through faith, is an event which took place within the history of Israel: through the life and passion, the death and resurrection, of Jesus of Nazareth (Yeshu ha-Noṣri), God has concluded a new covenant with the world. For Christianity, this belief has the same absolute status which the covenant of Sinai has for Israel. The Church can no more possess Israel's fundamental knowledge of itself and its salvation than a Jew can understand from within the essence of Christianity and share in it. But when they appeal to what has encountered them in their separate experiences, both Jew and Christian know that the revelation which has come to each—and come in a different way to each—is truth which comes from God. As a supranational *corpus mysticum,* teaching and conquering all nations, the Church of the Gospel, which calls itself the Church of the New Covenant, has a history. Likewise, Israel has a history, which has remained to the present day necessarily the history of the seed of Abraham. Within the particular knowledge and mission which has been granted to each, Christian and Jew confess the *same* God (creator, revealer, and savior of the world), as well as the same holy will of God, the fulfillment of which is awaited by both as the coming of the future kingdom.

Therefore, "the absolute in religious history" is this one unchangeable God, who has revealed his truth in diverse ways. But the truth is *one* truth, although the modes of participation in the truth differ. It is absolutely valid for Israel and for Christianity, for each according to the aspect which God has shown: to Israel upon Sinai, and to the world upon Golgotha. For the one who declared his name to Moses as "I am that I am" is the *one* eternal God, in all the variety of his revelations. Fully and absolutely he will remain to the Jews the same God that once looked with gracious favor upon them; fully and absolutely he is and will remain to the Christians the same God who became their God in another manner of mediation. Jews and Christians cannot and must not abandon the absolute claim laid upon them by their separate witnesses to the truth. Therefore, by the revealed will of divine predestination, they go their separate ways through history, parallel to each other. But as Christians and Jews, they know that in the supernatural future of the Kingdom of God, the parallels will intersect, and the two ways will be but one way —will be, indeed, no longer a way, but the goal.

These ways extend through time. A distance of some nineteen hundred years has already been covered. We do not know how many earthly years God will permit to elapse before earthly time will come to an end. But time is historical time, and the ways, too, have their history. In the course of this history, as a consequence of the dialectics of antagonism, Israel and Christianity have had differences of belief and faith. For most of the period up to the present, these have been differences in the etymological sense: separation from each other, justification of one's own belief, and refutation of the other's. Only for an incomparably shorter time have both sides attempted to enter into a conversation in which each really speaks and listens to the other. In what follows, we shall attempt, first of all, to follow the course of these differences from conflict of dogma to conversation between faiths. We shall examine the course of their historical and religious development, even if only in outline. We can base our plan for this history of theological controversy on many sources of Jewish written tradition which have scarcely been evaluated up to now. Their explication will give a firm doctrinal basis to the historical presentation. All the apocryphal, patristic, scholastic, and Reformation documents must remain beyond our scope. There is hope that this source material, even more voluminous, may also be approached from the Christian side, in order to write the same history of the Judaeo-Christian encounter.

This may suffice as a first step toward elucidating the basic presuppositions of this study. At the end we shall return once more to this subject. On the basis of these presuppositions, an attempt is made here for the first time to discuss so weighty and imposing a subject as nineteen centuries of Judaeo-Christian religious dialogue. The traditional party positions, of course, cannot take seriously this way of phrasing the question, nor see the whole force of its difficulty. For the most part, such a difficulty does not even occur to the uncompromisingly orthodox adherents of any religion. Such a person—seeing as he is himself possessed of absolute truth—accuses the rest of the world of error or at least lack of understanding. He simply lacks the inner readiness to engage in conversation truly receptive to the concern of anyone else. In the case of the religious liberal of any confession (at least insofar as his liberalism is merely the result of an antidogmatic affect), it usually happens that the unique element in the course of development, the revelation in religious history, threatens to vanish from sight. The antitheses tend to be submerged in some sort of synthesis, however questionable it may be. But today an attempt is being made to liquidate the theological inheritance of the nineteenth century; concurrently, the old religious parties are becoming less and less influential. If appearances are not deceptive, there is now a third possibility—new and open to both Jew and Christian—on the basis of which there exist the conditions necessary for genuine religious dialogue, dialogue which can be carried on with the full rigor of dogmatic theology, yet without resort to medieval nominalism.

If there is anything which this age demands, if there is anything which gives reason for hope, it is this: Christian and Jew, each within the common religious dialogue and also independent of it, each faithful to his own belief and his own way of life, bear common witness together before the world that they possess tidings from the divine realm; they go through history as corporeal evidence of the truth of God. The true line of progress of their conflict is often veiled. They carry it on against, with, and for each other. Its development passes from argument to dialogue, and will finally cease only when the time is fulfilled. Confronted with a world which for two centuries now has set itself against the word of God, per se, to a degree which increases terrifyingly, the Church and Israel—each in its proper way and in its place—have a common witness to bear: at *all* times, even contrary to appearances, God remains king over the whole earth.

II

ISRAEL
AND MANKIND

ONE of the most ancient accusations leveled again and again against the Jews in the course of history is their hostility toward non-Jewish mankind, especially toward Christianity. Reading the sources for the history of the first centuries after Christ, one can actually see that within the *Imperium Romanum,* even well into the fifth century, there was a bitter struggle for religious supremacy being waged between Judaism and Christianity. This exceedingly tense and fluctuating conflict, in which the Jews seemed temporarily to triumph, around 361, under the Emperor Julian is still far too little known, as is the extent of Jewish missionary propaganda, even in that period. These facts are extremely important for evaluating the historical fate of Judaism.[1] It is only since that time that the familiar Jewish position of historical impotence, that is, lack of power within secular history, has become decisive. This has been true down to this day, and will probably remain so until the end of time. From that period of struggle (a fact once more known only to a few) comes the majority of charges brought against Judaism up to this very day, from the charge of ritual murder, through the idea that on Purim the Saviour of the Christian religion is burned, to the charge that Jews are encouraged to defraud Gentiles, to revile them, to look upon them as cattle, and so forth. These allegations have been supported not only by many a passage from the Talmud torn out of context or wrongly understood and mistranslated, but also by many a hostile remark actually made and handed down in the debates of the Babylonian and Palestinian academies. These latter passages refer solely to concrete historical situations, and very often represent only too comprehensible emotional reactions to persecution and oppression of all kinds. These passages cannot be understood at all without intimate knowledge of Late Roman and Byzantine history. Certainly they are completely unsuitable for presenting a clear and valid picture of the actual teaching of the Jews, as is contained in the religious laws concerning the fate of the Gentiles and the Jewish attitude toward them. What Ismar Elbogen (MGWJ, 1936, pp. 47 f.) saw as a difficulty for all studies in the realm of comparative religion is fundamentally true for the citation of rabbinic statements: in contrast to the documents of the New Testament canon and patristic literature, which were written for a specific purpose or dealt with a specific point, the corpus of rabbinic literature "is a great reservoir of all possible utterances, of very different periods and places of origin, to a great extent brought together by chance. The existence of an individual statement is not determinative for the view of the whole." The intention is not to restrict the use of rabbinic-Talmudic material, but merely to cast the necessary light upon the indispensable precondition of knowledge based on the history of religion and lack of prejudice. For this reason, we shall proceed *ab ovo*. By way of introduction, we shall give, in brief compass, a presentation of the Jewish doctrine of the relationship of the Jews to the nations of the world, and especially to the Christians. This doctrine, as *halakhah,* must be considered fixed. In the following chapter, the actual conflict of faith between Israel and Christianity will be exhibited through Jewish literature of the first centuries. Then we shall pursue, on an historical basis, the development of the Jewish attitude toward Christianity and evaluation of it through the Middle Ages and into the nineteenth century. The last section will discuss the present, especially the endeavors of Martin Buber and Franz Rosenzweig—the historical juxtaposition of Israel and Christianity, a mystery which will be revealed only at the end of time.

The relationship of Israel to mankind takes as its first and foremost principle the fact that, according to the account of the Torah, all men are descended from one father. All of them, not as races or nations, but as *men,* are brothers in Adam, and are, therefore, called *benê Âdhâm* (sons of Adam) or *benê Nôah* (sons of Noah, Noachidae), since, after the flood, Noah, as representative of the principle of law, was preserver of the world. From the time of the occupation of Canaan down to the present day, the treatment of every stranger sojourning in the midst of an Israelite community has been determined by the prescription of Sinai: "And a stranger shalt thou not oppress; for ye know the heart of a stranger, seeing ye were strangers in the land of Egypt," (Exod. 23:9) and the Talmud states (Ḥagigah 5a): "Should anyone turn aside the right of the stranger, it is as though he were to turn aside the right of the most high God." In the extensive biblical legislation dealing with aliens, the stranger —*gêr* (sojourner), or *nokhrî* (foreigner), to use the biblical expression—sojourning in the land, whom you are to love as yourselves (Deut. 10:19), is equated legally and politically with the Israelite. Every stranger dwelling in the land has the possibility of becoming an Israelite in the full sense. Even the exception made by the Torah in the case of the Ammonites and Moabites (Deut. 23:4) was abolished by the Tannaim of the first century (Mishnah Yadayim IV, 4 and Berakot 28a) on interesting grounds: since the wars and conquests of Sennacherib, the differences between nations have been obliterated by intermarriage. Among the "proselytes" of the Jewish religious community in Palestine—as the Septuagint translated the biblical *gêrîm*—rabbinic literature differentiated the *gêr ṣedheḳ,* the full proselyte, who had himself circumcised and assumed the entire "yoke of the law," and the *gêr tôshâbh,* the stranger in the gate, the non-participating or semiproselyte, who lived in the land and, according to his free choice, assumed only a portion of the Jewish law as binding upon him. The solicitation of proselytes had been carried on systematically in the course of Jewish missionary propaganda ever since the time of the Babylonian exile, especially during the Maccabaean age and continuing into the fifth century. It was held by many to be a meritorious work. Thus Rabbi Simon ben Eleazar (Tanna of the second generation, about 130) states: "The Holy One, blessed be he, gave Israel over into *gâlûth* [exile, dispersion] among the nations only in order that they might attract to themselves proselytes." (Pesaḥim 87b) Only after unfortunate experiences with proselytes became common was greater care taken. After the third century, more voices were raised against the institution of proselytes. (Rabbi Ḥelbo: "For the Jews, proselytes are as grievous as leprosy.") (Yebamot 47b) The aftereffects of the persecution under Hadrian (A.D. 135), the deterioration of the world situation for the Jews, the growth of the fence about the law, the decision of the rabbis to make conversion difficult (Yebamot 47a: "The rabbis taught: If anyone in the present day wishes to become a proselyte, let him be asked: what leads you to become a proselyte? Do you not know that the people of Israel in the present day are afflicted, dispersed, humiliated, robbed, that suffering is their lot?")—all these reasons made conversions rarer and rarer during the following period, but they have taken place in every century. The best known is the case of the Khazars, a Tatar people living in the Crimea, who, following the example of their royal house, were in large measure converted about 770.

Michael Guttmann[2] has described in detail the significant transformation which the above-mentioned concept of the "stranger within the gate," or "semiproselyte" underwent in the centuries after Christ. Referring to these people, the Greek and Latin documents of the period took over the Hebrew phrase *yir'ê adhônay,* calling them "god-fearers." In Hellenistic Judaism this name was attached to the heathen in the Diaspora who joined in the Jewish form of worship, occasionally visiting the Synagogues, but for the most part without observing the ceremonial laws and without being reckoned in the company of the Jewish congregation.[3] In the course of this period, the concept of the god-fearer became increasingly and more generally a means of distinguishing between Gentiles. Whoever kept the Noachite laws—that is, the laws known to Noah and pre-Israelite mankind—was called a god-fearer. In the discussion of these laws set forth in Sanhedrin 56 (of the Babylonian Talmud), they are determined to be the prohibition of idolatry, blasphemy, unchastity, shedding of blood, robbery, and eating the flesh of living animals, together with the commandment of responsibility. Maimonides formulated the true Jewish conception, held to and proclaimed by tradition in all periods, in Mishnah Torah IV, Hilkot Melakim, Section X, Halakhah 2: "Whoever professes to obey the seven Noachite laws and strives to keep them is classed with the devout among the Gentiles, and has a share in the world to come." It is of course true, according to Maimonides (*ibid.,* VIII, 11), that only that man is to be accounted a "devout Gentile" who fulfills these laws, not as dictated by reason, but because of his awareness of their divine origin. With this important restriction: every individual who keeps the Noachite laws is set on a par with the Jews. Indeed, a statement made by Rabbi Meir (*ca.* A.D. 150) is even recorded three times in the Talmud: "The pagan who concerns himself with the teaching of God is like to the High Priest." (Sanhedrin 59a; Baba Kamma 38a; and 'Aboda Zarah 36a)

Whatever may have been the origin of the political institution of the *gêr tôshâbh,* the semiproselyte, or "stranger within the gate," it fell into desuetude when the Jubilee Year ceased to exist in its full legal form, that is, ever since Israel ceased to exist as a nation. Understandably, the Noachidae occupied the places left vacant by the "devout among the Gentiles." Through their "righteousness," which is not solely the inheritance of the congregation of Jacob, they also have a share in the world to come (Tosefta Sanh. 13, 2; Bamidbar Rabbah 8, 2; and elsewhere). The Talmudic literature does not employ a specific designation for Christians; the term *mînîm* (heretics) is invariably applied only to Jewish heretics (among whom, of course, the Jewish Christians were counted), concerning whom many a harsh judgment can be found. "Among the Gentiles there are no *mînîm*," says the Talmud (Ḥullin 13b). The later designation for Christianity in religious law is *shittûph,* that is, "ascribing the name of God to something else." The medieval commentators made this clear (especially in commentaries on tractate Sukkah 45b, which discusses *shittûph*) by distinguishing Christian worship clearly from *abhôdhâh zârâh* (idolatry), thereby recognizing it indirectly as a possibility within the Noachite laws.[4] Therefore, the Tossafot to Sanhedrin 63b, Megillah 28a, Bekorot 2b, Shulḥan 'Aruḥ O. C. 156, and other passages declare that Jews are permitted to allow a Christian to swear a Christian oath before them, even though *shittûph* occurs and another is being addressed with the honor due to God.

Medieval literature also contains numerous direct definitions, decisions, replies, and so forth,[5] specifying the position Christianity occupies vis-à-vis Jewish religious law. Maimonides states (Pe'er ha-Dor 50): "The Christians believe and confess, as do we, that the Bible is of divine origin and was revealed to our teacher Moses; only in interpretation of Scripture do they differ."[6] And we read in a letter of Maimonides to his pupil Ḥasdai ha-Levi, which has been cited frequently against interpretation hostile to Judaism: "In regard to your question concerning the (Gentile) nations, you should know that God demands the *heart,* that matters are to be judged according to the intent of the heart. There is, therefore, no doubt that everyone (from among the Gentiles) who brings his soul to perfection through virtues and wisdom in the knowledge of God has a share in eternal blessedness."

Ever since S. F. Brenz's *Abgestreifter jüdischer Schlangenbalg (The Jewish Snake-skin Sloughed)*, published in 1614, and Johann Eisenmenger's *Entdecktes Judentum (Judaism Revealed)*, published in 1700, many passages have been used by anti-Semites to "demonstrate" occasions of hatred and curses directed against Christians. In regard to these, we shall cite a statement of Rabbi Eliezer Ashkenazi (1580; quoted by Zunz, *op. cit.*, p. 385): "Even when we curse those who injure us unjustly and inflict evil upon us, this curse—

God forbid!—is no precept of religion, but rather it is like the action of any man who, having been wronged, curses his son or his brother. Far be it from us to curse an entire nation, even when a portion of it has done us wrong." Ultimately, in spite of all resignation to the will of God, the Jews of the Middle Ages could react only as *men* to unjust afflictions, gruesome persecutions, and pogroms. With fearful heart, they complained before God of their suffering in exile (cf. the next chapter). But they knew very well how to distinguish those who act after the manner of Edom from those who do not act after the manner of Edom ('Abodah Zarah 10h), the idolators and the god-fearers among the Gentiles. Thus, several passages of Shulḥan 'Aruḥ set forth strict boundaries separating pagan idolatry from Christian iconolatry. Be'er ha-Golah, a collection of supplementary writings of Rabbi Moses Ribkas (1640), included in many editions of Shulḥan 'Aruh, states expressly in regard to *ḥoshen ha-mishpaṭ* (p. 266, par. 1; and p. 425, par. 5): "Everything which the Talmud says about the *gôyîm* refers to the previous nations, who were idolaters. But the nations in whose midst we live hold to many of the major tenets of our religion. They worship the creator of heaven and earth. It is our duty to pray for their authorities. . . ." This view is shared by almost all authorities, and is stated at every appropriate opportunity.

This point is strongly emphasized because the Torah has decreed extermination as the punishment for idolatry (Deut. 7, and elsewhere). Many passages in the Talmud which set up standards for the conduct of Jews toward idolators were mistakingly construed by anti-Semites of later periods as referring to Gentiles of their own day. Insofar as the Gentile world is Christian (and also Mohammedan), Jewish religious law places it within the realm of *shittûph*, i.e., the adulteration of the Jewish faith with non-Jewish elements. In spite of

all differences, the Jews share with Christians (and Moham-
medans) belief in the same God, the God of Israel, whom
Scripture also acknowledges to be "God of the nations." (Jer.
10:7; Isa. 2:3; Pss. 47:8, 82:8; and elsewhere) The God of
Israel is at the same time the God who cares for the Gentile
world. "Have we not all one father? Hath not one God created us?" asks the prophet Malachi (2:10). From the awareness of this fact has flowed many a conversation and many a
community of mission and destiny, both historically and in
the present, following the rhythm of historical religious development. From antiquity to the present, the charge of "mis-
anthropy" has been leveled against Israel again and again,
even by Christianity, although the relationship of the Jews to
the world about them at all times has been strictly regulated,
both religiously and in practice, and this relationship has been
easily discoverable by anyone willing to find it out.[7] If we are
correct, this charge has its ultimate roots in a profound misunderstanding of the fact that Israel is the "chosen people."
This inability of the Gentiles to understand has a metaphysical significance which we shall discuss later. The real answer
is given by the Midrash Yalḳuṭ Shim'oni on Psalm 109:4:
" 'In return for my love they are my adversaries' "—so speaks
Israel to the Gentiles. " 'You should love us, for we have presented seventy sacrifices for you;[8] but you did not love us, but
rather hated us—and yet we pray for you.' "

III

THE FIRST CENTURIES OF CONFLICT

T HE anti-Semitic polemic of the nations of the world goes back to early antiquity—to be exact, to Haman's vexation that here was a nation with laws differing from the law of every nation. Similarly, the arguments of Christian polemic against Judaism have been the same for over nineteen centuries; they can be traced back to the earliest period of history of the Christian Church. They consist of the following statements, belonging to the doctrinal basis of *every* Christian Church, proclaimed in all centuries by the Church's theology. They refer to the fact of Christian might and Jewish historical impotence, in ever-repeated exegeses of certain Old Testament passages.

1. The Messiah, foretold in Genesis 49:10, Isaiah 53, and numerous other passages of Scripture, was Jesus of Nazareth, who was nailed to the cross under Pontius Pilate.

2. Since the rejection and crucifixion of the Messiah, Jesus of Nazareth, the election of Israel has been transferred to the

Christian Church; henceforth the Church is to be called the true Israel.

3. The punishment resulting from the crucifixion of Jesus is the destruction of the Jerusalem temple. This is an expression of God's consequent rejection of the people of Israel, who, because of their hardness of heart, must wander through the world until the Lord's return. Then all Israel will be converted, enter into knowledge of Jesus, and find salvation through him.

4. According to the witness of Paul, the Jewish law has been abrogated through faith in the new revelation.

Jews of all centuries have bitterly contested all four statements. The growing Church was not taken seriously during the first centuries of this era. For this reason, remarkably few passages can be found in the Talmud referring indisputably to the historical Jesus;[9] and the knowledge which the Babylonian rabbis had in general of the whole course of events in Galilee was scanty and legendary. In the following centuries, which saw the Church attain the status of a world power, dogmatic controversies were, as a rule, avoided, provided there was no compulsion to take an explicit stand. In spite of this, there is much material—naturally, mostly haggadic—for the discussion of doctrinal questions. This material, in its extent and diffusion, can hardly be overlooked. The dialogues of the scholars of the Talmud, the Tannaim and Amoraim, are always based on concrete circumstances and often resemble modern parliamentary debates. In attacking heretical notions, they were frequently concerned to refute Christian doctrines, especially when the latter—like the previously mentioned four points—cast doubt to such a degree upon the justification of Israel's continued historical existence as a nation. The midrashim compiled in Talmudic times, and particularly those of more recent recension, together with the Yalkut, are full of material pertinent to these questions. In this limited space we must relinquish historical interpretation of the individual sources;[10] out of the vast supply of material, we shall give the Jewish replies to Christian doctrines, insofar as they are of more than temporary significance. It is precisely in these replies that the Jewish self-awareness of the ages is reflected. Since this whole domain of scholarship stands in need of systematic treatment, our rehearsal of the Jewish response to early Christianity shall be summary.[11] The answers given by the rabbis of the first centuries[12] for the support and instruction of the people reveal, basically, neither more nor less than the mystery of Israel: *why* the Jews all bear the sufferings of exile, wandering through the ages, neither perishing nor submitting to baptism, but, as the covenant community of God, conveying to mankind a message which yet today remains sealed with the name of the Lord—blessed be his name—which is called *truth*.

1 THE MESSIAHSHIP OF JESUS

So-called "scriptural proof," based on the Old Testament, has always had immense importance for both Christians and Jews. Such proofs are comprehensible to men of today only when they consider that the Bible has been a document not only of revelation, history, and law, but also of prophecy. In it, future events are already anticipated by way of suggestion or by type—typological exegesis. For example, in the fate of the Patriarchs is seen that of their descendants; Edom, according to the *Haggadah,* is of the type of Rome and so forth. Early Christian congregations had every incentive to interpret specific passages in such a way that they would refer to Jesus; for example, Isaiah 7:14, which describes the birth of a descend-

ant of David by the name Immanuel, is thought to have been
Jesus. The messenger of the Lord in Malachi 3:1 is seen as
John the Baptist, representing Elijah, and thus predecessor of
the Nazarene. Similarly, the 110th Psalm is seen as containing
a prophecy of the heavenly tribunal, with Jesus sitting at the
right hand of God. There are many other such passages. Jewish scholars replied to such exegesis by referring the passages
in question to other historical events, often to King Heze-
kiah; but the Christological exegeses of the Church Fathers
(in spite of the school of historical criticism), mediated by
medieval literature, have been taken over by Christian theology of our own day.[13]

The form of demonstration peculiar to early Christianity
was to build everything upon the word of the Bible, proving every statement with biblical quotations, ignoring in
the process the context in which the quotation was located
or giving any consideration to the historical conditions
under which it was written. This process certainly witnesses
to the absolute sovereignty and exclusive authority of Scripture; but, in this "naïve" form, it cannot be adopted by
our present mode of thought. J. Ziegler (*ibid.*, pp. 64 f.)
correctly points out that the persuasive power of the Gospel
can be rightly understood only when the skill with which the
new doctrine assimilated this method of proof is properly
recognized. The Christian reader of today, out of touch with
this "Jewish" thought pattern, can only rarely give this fact its
due. This is especially so when—Strack-Billerbeck notwith-
standing—he does not give close enough attention to references to the corresponding passages of Scripture or parallels
in the contemporary writings of the rabbis, and the *specific*
recasting of common Jewish doctrines of the period. The following examples may serve here to illustrate the method of
scriptural proof: Jesus was born in Bethlehem, and is accord-

ingly the Messiah, *for* it is written in the prophet Micah (5:1) "But thou, Bethlehem . . . Out of thee shall one come forth unto Me that is to be ruler in Israel." (Matt. 2:5 f.) Jesus was in Egypt for a time, and is accordingly God's Son, *for* we read in Hosea 11:1: "Out of Egypt I called My son." (Matt. 2:15) Jesus rides into Jerusalem upon an ass, *for* it says in Zechariah 9:9: "Behold, thy king cometh unto thee . . . Lowly, and riding upon an ass." (Matt. 21:5) Jesus innocently suffered much, and accordingly he is the Messiah, *for* Isaiah teaches (53:4): "Surely our diseases he did bear, and our pains he carried." (Matt. 8:17) This recurrent appeal to prophecy was either a so-called *vaticinium post eventum* (prophecy after the event), with the event itself inserted into the life of Jesus in order subsequently to confirm the word of the prophet; or, conversely according to the principle *leḳayyêm mâh shenê'-emâr;* that is, in order to fulfill what is written, Jesus conformed his acts to prophetic statement. Whichever it may be, recognition of this exegetic device confirms that the proponents of the new doctrine conducted their disputes quite in the Jewish manner. Much emphasis is placed upon these conclusions, because to a degree which cannot be overlooked, they contribute to the reading of the New Testament as *Haggadah*. Long passages of the New Testament are, indeed, actually nothing less than *new and different exegesis* of the Jewish Bible, the difference being determined by belief in the divine sonship of Jesus. It is thus already a "justification" of *the* Scriptures.[14]

Of decisive importance in this process of "biblical proof" (which the Church Fathers found highly developed among the Alexandrian Jews and ready to be put to their own use) was the vision of the Suffering Servant of God (*'ebhedh ha-shêm*) in Isaiah 52-53. The Church interpreted this as referring to Jesus, and declared the prophecy to have been fulfilled through his passion and death. For the most part, the rabbis replied by deeming the entire nation of Israel to be the Suffering Servant, an interpretation which the Church Father Origen records in *Contra Celsum* as the view of a Jewish scholar. The rabbis saw Israel's historical destiny of suffering predicted here, declaring that the Suffering Servant passages had nothing to do with Jesus or even with the Messiah. That Israel was intended by Isaiah to be a suffering missionary remained the pervading interpretation of the majority of Jewish biblical exegetes of the Middle Ages (Rashi, Ibn Ezra, David Kimḥi, *et al.*).

Christological doctrine in itself—the belief that God has become man and has allowed his only-begotten son to suffer sacrificial death as a propitiation for the sins of mankind—has remained, as Paul rightly says, a "stumbling block" to the Jews. It is an impossible article of belief, which detracts from God's sovereignty and absolute otherness—an article which, in fact, destroys the world.[15] Indeed, the Sadducean High Priest (heeding the rabbinic directive on the conduct of a judge upon hearing blasphemy) rended his clothing in horror at the assertion of an incarnation of the eternal God. Similarly, according to Acts 7:54-60, when Stephen confessed his faith in the heavenly Son of God, he was stoned. It is the same passionate belief which can be heard in an admittedly late homiletical midrash: "It is not permitted a human mouth to say, 'The Holy One—blessed be he—has a son.' If God could not look on in anguish while Abraham sacrificed his son, would he then have suffered his own son to be killed, without destroying the entire world?" (Agadah Bereshit 31) And in another passage: When Nebuchadnezzar used the expression, " 'He is like a son of the gods' " (Dan. 3:25), an angel came down from heaven, smote him on the mouth, and said, "Blasphemer! Does God then have a son?' " (T. J. Shab-

bat 8; similarly, Midr. Samuel V, 7) Further, Midrash Rabbah explains, in reference to Exodus 20:2: " 'I am the Lord
thy God': Compare therewith a king of flesh and blood. He
reigns, and has a father or a brother or a son. The Holy One—
blessed be his name—said, I am not so. 'I am the first,' for I
have no father; 'and I am the last,' for I have no son; 'beside
Me there is no God' (Isa. 44:6), for I have no brother." (R.
Abbahu, an Amora of the second generation, prior to 300)[16]

In matters of Christology, we can attach more weight to the
material preserved by the Tannaitic sources which can be referred in the narrower sense to the historical Jesus. Such
material consists of a few scattered notices—incidental remarks which, as is often the case in the Talmud, are inexact
and uncertain in regard to their historical significance. They
admit only the conclusion that the early Tannaim did not
think the events around the year of Jesus' death to be especially important; in that period, proponents of irregular
doctrines and convictions based on messianic heresy were
not unusual. The only item of importance is that Yeshu ha-
Noṣri is called (using an idiom common at that time) a man
who "burned his food in public," that is, caused a public scandal, became an apostate (Sanh. 103a, and elsewhere). His
views are recorded because he ridiculed the words of the wise
(according to Matt. 23), led the people of Israel astray, and
induced them to apostasy (Sanh. 43a; 107b; Soṭah 47b).[17]
Only at the close of the tannaitic era, about two centuries after
the crucifixion, does R. Eliezer ha-Ḳappar, a contemporary
of the rabbi who was redactor of the Mishnah—plainly influenced by discussions with Gentile Christians—accuse Jesus
of elevating himself to the status of divinity (according to
Yalḳuṭ Shim'oni 765 on Num. 23:7). As justification for this
charge, a decisive objection (in the Jewish view of that period) was raised against any possible messiahship on the
part of Jesus: the possibility of referring the crucifixion to the

passage in the Torah, "he that is hanged is a reproach unto God." (Deut. 21:23) The fatal import of this statement also made great difficulty for Paul (Gal. 3:13). The much-cited "scandal of the cross" hinges on this passage!

Rabbinic passages of the above-mentioned kind can be found with others collected *in toto* by Joseph Klausner, as well as by the Christian theologians Heinrich Laible, Gustaf Dalman, and Hermann Strack. It must be emphasized once more that these are incidental remarks, which never assumed central importance. They are of value to the historian of religion who wishes to obtain information about the intellectual climate of the period and gain familiarity with the peculiarities of polemic of that time. The attitude of present-day Judaism—as remains to be shown—has altered decisively, and these statements possess *no* normative force. This whole process of free midrashic exegesis is found among the Amoraim and also, as a pattern of thought, among the Church Fathers; it is important solely for the light it casts on the historical doctrinal convictions of the time.

Only after the growing Church began to develop a Christological doctrine—that is, after the middle of the third century—do we find such statements of the Amoraim, thus motivated, concerning the doctrine of the incarnate God. These are intended to illustrate the impossibility of Christological doctrine for strict Jewish transcendental monotheism. As the passages referred to show, this doctrine ultimately had to be rejected as being quite impossible, given the basis of the Jewish experience of God. God, who is without form, cannot be incorporated in any shape, no matter how fashioned; without boundary and prior to all form, it is he who creates forms. No rabbinic exegete ever felt it necessary to enter into a discussion of the content of Pauline teaching. Christian soteriology restricted the distinctive mark of the Jewish nation, the *'ebhedh ha-shêm,* to a single individual who suffers vicariously as a propitiation for the sins of his fellow men, being therein and thereby the Messiah. To the rabbis, this must have seemed just so much "Greek" speculation. Had a Jew propounded such a doctrine as being *the* meaning of the Torah, according to the Jewish way of thinking he would thereby have surrendered the true meaning and content of revealed monotheistic religion. Furthermore, this un-Jewish shift of ideas contradicted all the realistic expectations of the "messianic age" shared by that period, from Judas Maccabeus to Simon bar Kokhba. This age was to bring a real end to Roman oppression, together with peace on earth under the victorious scepter of the royal Messiah, as well as the supernatural miracle of cessation of sin. Above all, the royal Messiah was expected to be a human being. The postexilic name for the Messiah, *ben' âdhâm* ("son of man"), which occurs especially in the book of Daniel, was obviously formed in contradistinction to ideas of a "Son of God" common among contemporary pagans. It was intended as an anti-mythological Jewish term. It is true, however, that these pagan conceptions penetrated into the messianic doctrine of the apocalyptic books of the first century after Christ, especially IV Ezra.

A final word on the idea that the devout believer—including and, in particular, the one sent by God—must suffer *as a man*. This opinion is and was well known to Judaism. This was the reason that the Jews of the fourth century could enter into political alliance with the Arian Christians, who acknowledged the human Jesus, but denied his divinity. The idea that God becomes man, suffers of his own free will, and is defeated by the evil of the world—this is an impossibility for Judaism! Of course, it is no secret that even the Talmud speaks of a suffering forerunner Messiah (e.g., in Sukkah 52a), the Messiah ben Joseph, of the tribe of Ephraim, who is even defeated in battle and killed. Only then after his

death, does the Messiah ben David appear, who will bring
final deliverance. This doctrine developed only very late (according to G. Kittel, certainly no earlier than the second century). It can be viewed as a reflected answer to the question of
the Messiah as newly stated by the Christians—an attempt to
connect the demonstration of the Messiah's power with the
problem of suffering. It was not, however, the *figure* of the
Messiah which became decisive for later Judaism, but rather
the earthly *kingdom* expected for the messianic age, in which
"the Lord shall be King over all the earth; In that day shall
the Lord be One, and His name one." (Zech. 14:9)

2 THE ELECTION OF ISRAEL

The second attack which the young Church directed
against the Synagogue was aimed at the Holy Scriptures
themselves: specifically, against all the passages of the Torah
which teach the election of the nation Israel.[18] The Church
did not fashion its attack after the manner of the pagan, who
had throughout been scandalized by this claim. Ignorant of
the power of God, who has mercy upon whom he has mercy,
paganism interpreted the election as nationalistic presump-
tion or even as a Jewish claim to domination of the world.
Possibly this conception could even have been elicited from
the naïve pride present in many passages of the Talmud.
But the Deuteronomist had already replied that, as a nation,
Israel had not been chosen by God because it was more in
number (*sc.* mightier) than any other nation (Deut. 7:7).[19]
According to Scripture, this election is spiritual, but it is to be
understood realistically. God has chosen as his possession one
of the nations of the earth, and called it to represent his royal
will: "Ye shall be Mine own treasure from among all peoples;

for all the earth is Mine; and ye shall be unto Me a kingdom of priests, and a holy nation." (Exod. 19:5-6) To this summons is joined a condition: "If ye will hearken unto My voice indeed, and keep My covenant."

The most immediate course for the polemic of the Church was to demonstrate that this condition had been broken by the sins of Israel. Israel's expulsion from the Land of Promise, her dispersion and wretched estate were clearly an expression of divine rejection. Do we not already see fulfilled, the Church asks, the threats of punishment contained in the Torah: "But it shall come to pass, if thou wilt not hearken unto the voice of the Lord thy God, to observe to do all His commandments and His statutes which I command thee this day; that all these curses shall come upon thee, and overtake thee" (Deut. 28:15); and in the Prophets: "You only have I known of all the families of the earth; therefore I will visit upon you all your iniquities." (Amos 3:2) The Apostle Paul, especially, never tires of declaring that "God's wrath has come upon them at last," for they are those who "killed both the Lord Jesus and the prophets, and drove us out, and displease God and oppose all men." Therefore, "you, brethren, became imitators of the churches of God in Christ Jesus which are in Judaea." (I Thess. 2:14-16) Henceforth the election of Israel has been transferred to the people of the Christian Church; the Christians are now the children of promise (Gen. 18:10), the true seed of Abraham (Rom. 9:7 f.); and I Peter declares, using the words of the Torah, "You are a chosen race, a royal priesthood, a holy nation, God's own people," and so forth (2:9). This connection of the crucifixion of Jesus with the rejection of the Jews and the transfer of Israel's election to the Christian Church, as the legitimate heir determined by God, is stated as an item of dogma by all the Church Fathers, demonstrated by them from Scripture,[20] brought forward in numerous disputations by Christian theologians of the Middle Ages as a threatening *argumentum ad hominem,* and held to the present day as a doctrine of the church.[21]

What, then, did the teachers of the Synagogue have to say in reply? First of all: they disagreed violently with what they believed to be the Christian misinterpretation of Holy Scripture. Having foreseen the possibility of such misinterpretation, God had given a twofold teaching: in addition to that set down in writing, there was also an oral tradition, without which the Torah could not be understood at all.[22] Bamidbar Rabbah, chapter 14 (interpreting Hos. 8:12) states: "The oral tradition was not given in writing, lest the Gentiles should falsify it, as they have done with the written tradition, then asserting that they are Israel. Therefore God said to Hosea: "though I write for him never so many things of My Law, They are accounted as a stranger's." God also denied Moses' request to reduce the Mishnah to writing, because he foresaw that the Gentiles would translate the Scriptures into Greek and say, We are Israel (R. Judah ben Shalom, in Tanḥ. Wayera 5—directed against such statements as the one in Justin's *Dialogue with Trypho,* 11). In Shabbat 116, interpreting a legal passage from the Torah, the appeal of the wife of Rabbi Eliezer in conversation with a philosopher is to be taken as a reply to the Church's claim to have entered into its inheritance as daughter of Israel: "When there is a son, the daughter may not inherit."

In all ages, the Jewish faith has viewed possession of the Torah as the guarantee of its secure election. For ages, the Jews have expressed their deepest understanding of themselves in the daily Benediction of the Torah: "Blessed art Thou, O Lord, our God, King of the Universe, who hast chosen us from among all nations and hast given us thy precepts." The Pirke Abot relates the saying of R. Akiba that the Israelites are called God's children, as was declared to them out of God's special love. And further: "Beloved are the Israelites, for a special instrument has been granted them. Out of special love, it was declared to them that a precious instrument had been granted to them, through which the world was created." For it is written in Proverbs 4:2: "For I give you good doctrine; forsake ye not my teaching." (III, 18) One of the Tannaim, a mystic by the name of R. Simeon b. Yoḥai, spoke of the nearness of God to his chosen people, the reality of the union of his shekhinah with Israel even after the destruction of the temple: "Come and see how beloved to the Holy One, blessed be his name, are the Israelites. Wherever they were exiled, the shekhinah was with them. So it was in Egypt [there follows a reference to I Sam. 2:27], so it was in the Babylonian *gâlûth* [reference to Isa. 43:14], so it is in the Edomitic [Roman] *gâlûth* [reference to Isa. 63:1]. Even when they are finally delivered, the shekhinah will be with them, for it is written in Deuteronomy 30:3: 'The Lord thy God will turn thy captivity.' It is not written that he will bring it back, but will turn it back. This teaches that the shekhinah of the Holy One (blessed be his name!) will return with them from the *gâlûth*." (Megillah 29a)[23]

This and many other doctrinal statements of the Talmud, or interpretation of the Midrash (usually verifying the suggested exegesis with suitably selected passages from Scripture), quite obviously must be viewed as replies to Christian polemic. Israel remains the people of God; the covenant cannot be nullified. Thus the scholars reassure the nation. At the moment, the nation is in travail, but, in the first place, the evidence of such travail is not an admissible argument, since it is historical impotence which can demonstrate God's love;[24] in the second place, there is not the slightest causal relationship between the misery of the nation and the crucifixion of

Jesus, although presumably it is related to the punishments threatened in Scripture, if the people break the ordinances of the covenant and sin obtains the upper hand. In this other event, the Torah has promised, "the Lord shall scatter thee among all peoples, from the one end of the earth even unto the other end of the earth." (Deut. 28:64)

Starting with the ninth chapter of the Epistle to Barnabas and running through all patristic literature is the assertion on the part of Christian writers that Israel has been rejected by God because of the sin of the golden calf. If this is true, Israel replies: "If I appear so reprehensible on account of this single offence, how reprehensible must you be!" (Shir ha-Shirim Rabbah on 1:6, and elsewhere) But such verdicts are not man's to deliver, for no man knows God's decree. And the Christians do not have the right (so the rabbis assure us repeatedly), by means of their allegories, to interpret Scripture contrary to the sense of the words in order to "prove" the *rejection* of Israel, and in this manner claim the Election for the Church. What is revealed is revealed, and God is a God of truth. It is written in the Torah: "And yet for all that, when they are in the land of their enemies, I will not reject them, neither will I abhor them, to destroy them utterly, and to break My covenant with them; for I am the Lord their God." (Lev. 26:44)

That is the point: punishment, yes—but not rejection. The *gâlûth* is perhaps even a blessing for Israel; it assures the eternity of the nation.[25] That suffering would come upon Israel was predicted by the prophet Isaiah: "I have tried thee in the furnace of affliction." (48:10) The destruction of the temple and the dispersion among the Gentiles have their point of origin in the Election, and are compassed within the divine plan. This all came about *"ûmippenê haṭâ'ênû"* ("on account of our sins") and will endure until, at a future time, our destiny will be altered by divine mercy. If now the scoffers come and ask, Where is then the power of God, seeing as he does not punish the persecutors of Israel?, R. Joshua b. Levi (Amora of the first generation, about 320) answers: "This is his power, that he restrains his wrath and remains patient with blasphemers. These are his terrible deeds; for, without the terrible deeds of the Holy One (blessed be his name!), how could Israel continue to exist among all the nations of the world?" (Yoma 69b) In regard to the sufferings which afflict the Israelites here below: as repayment for the afflictions sent by God, they have promised to them in return the divine precepts, the Holy Land, and the world to come (Mekiltah on Exod. 20:3). Knowing this, the same Joshua b. Levi could even dare to say, "Not even a wall of iron can effect a separation between Israel and its Father in heaven." (Pesahim 85b)[26] And this deep conviction is paraphrased by another passage: "Even were all the nations of the earth to join together to put an end to God's love for Israel, they could not do so." (Shemot Rabbah)

3 THE DESTRUCTION OF THE TEMPLE

The destruction of the temple at the hand of Titus took place in the year 70. The final banishment of the Jews into the dispersion, the *gâlûth Rômî,* also called the Fourth Woe, or the Edomite captivity,[27] took place after the failure of Bar Kokhba and the fall of Betar, in 135. We have already mentioned that these events served the polemic of the Church during the first centuries as an especially impressive argument for its view of God's rejection of the Jews.[28] In particular, at the end of the second century, the Church Fathers elaborated a detailed theory in which the destruction of Jerusalem was to be understood as a punishment of God for the crucifixion of Jesus and as a fulfillment of the "Shiloh prophecy" of Genesis 49:10—henceforth the scepter has departed from Judah. Two hundred years later, Augustine even goes so far as to state that the Jews who were responsible for Jesus' crucifixion were less guilty than their successors, who would not believe in the divinity of Jesus enthroned in heaven (MPL 36, 859). This last charge can hardly have made any impression on the Jews, since, not believing in the Ascension of Jesus, they could hardly understand the Christian idea that the Son is enthroned in heaven beside the Father. In Sukkah 5a, Rabbi Jose speaks of the complete transcendence of heaven with respect to earth: "The Divinity has never come to earth, and Moses and Elijah never ascended into heaven; for it is written in Psalm 115:16, 'The heavens are the heavens of the Lord; but the earth hath He given to the children of men.' " In Sanhedrin 38b, Rabbi Idit writes in a similar vein.

As far as we can see, the Jewish writings of the first centuries gave no direct reply whatever to the statements of the Church Fathers. Probably it seemed to them so monstrous to construct a relationship between the crucifixion of Jesus of Nazareth and the destruction of the temple that they could only remain silent. As a result, the immediate impression of the catastrophe had all the more intense an effect, an effect which has remained unchanged down through the centuries to the present day. The explanations of the reasons for this disaster, and its meaning, had already received their final form in the three generations immediately subsequent to it. All that remained to their successors was to elaborate upon the theme. Any endeavor along this line which could lay claim to legitimacy from the Jewish point of view had to result in finding the basis of the catastrophe in the sin and guilt of the people and their fathers. God was exonerated of authorship, but traces of his redemptive purpose were discerned in the event. The reconstruction of the temple and its

sacrificial cultus were read out of the prophets as an event of
the messianic future.

Shabbat 119b gives eight different answers to the
question of *why* the temple was destroyed and the
miseries of exile brought upon the Jews. As Arthur
Marmorstein (*Religionsgeschichtliche Studien* II, pp. 111 f.)
has clearly shown, these had the homiletic purpose of com-
bating the Church doctrine that Jesus' death had been the
cause of the destruction of the temple and of the exile. These
are the reasons contained in the replies: (1) they had pro-
faned the Sabbath; (2) they had failed to recite the Shema'
every morning and evening; (3) they had neglected the instruction of their children; (4) they no longer had any fear
of evil; (5) they had made small and great equal; (6) they
did not admonish each other; (7) they looked down upon
the scribes; (8) men of faith had disappeared. Finally, in
another passage (Yoma 9b), the senseless mutual enmity of
the Jews of the period is given as the major reason for the
destruction of the second temple. This outweighed even the
three cardinal sins of idolatry, shedding of blood and unchastity.[29] But others (such as R. Johanan and R. Eleazar)
teach that, in contrast to the first destruction of the temple,
the sins which brought about the second were not revealed.
For this reason, the end of the fourth *gâlûth* cannot be predicted (Yoma 9b).

Certainly the destruction of the temple is the axis of Jewish
historical destiny. It brought to a halt the focus of religious
practice, the sacrificial worship;[30] for this reason, the centuries
of reflection which fasten upon this destruction can hardly be
scanned. These events ultimately lie in the mystery of divine
providence; however, every Jew who has taken a position
with regard to them has seen the cause of the catastrophe as
the abundant sins of the Jews, and the cause of the delay in

the coming of redemption as their perseverance in sin. This is *the* Jewish historical consciousness; indeed, it penetrated very early into the liturgy. The Amidah in the Musaf prayer, which was fixed in its present form in the course of the first centuries (cf. Ismar Elbogen, *Der jüdische Gottesdienst,* 1924, pp. 132 ff.), begins with this sentence: "On account of our sins we have been driven from our land and have entered upon misery; we have been banished from our soil—because of the hand which was stretched out against thy sanctuary."

The destruction of the temple, the cessation of the sacrificial cultus, the loss of political independence, and the burden of suffering in exile have at all times aroused natural emotions of honor and justice. But, in their deeper significance and true meaning, they have always been felt to be the result of sin. The Christians argued that the suffering which came upon the Jews was connected with the crucifixion of Christ; but this argument could not move the Jews, no matter how often in the course of the Middle Ages they were made to feel what could happen when the Church and its monastic orders aroused the masses. The Church taught that the only means of redemption for them was "conversion." Their understanding was different, and more in line with the teaching of the Bible: they read in the prophets of the "return" which God at all times demanded of them. If at all posible, the Jews of later centuries avoided the theme "Jesus is the Christ," because any statement they might make carried with it personal danger to their lives. According to their reading of history, in this matter they were free from sin (in rejecting and condemning Jesus, according to the Jewish law dealing with blasphemy in M. Sanhedrin VI, 4), however strong and universal Jewish awareness of sin has otherwise been.

The history of the *gâlûth* is the history of suffering. The sufferings inflicted upon the chosen people over the course of time are so great that God himself must weep over them (Berak. 3a; Ḥagigah 5b; and elsewhere). Without discounting periods of peace and transitory improvements, Jewish history from the fifth century on has been a history of persecutions and banishments. The Israelites held the firm conviction that they were God's people, and that their election was as valid today as it had ever been. In return for this, they accepted the martyrdom prepared for them by the Church of the Middle Ages because of their "hardness of heart." More than one pyre blazed; and the blood sacrifices of the Inquisition are without number.

In his haggadic commentary (Zebaḥ Pesaḥ), R. Isaac Abrabanel, one of the most important contemporaries of the expulsion of the Spanish Jews, writes (interpreting Ps. 118: 13): " 'Thou didst push me hard, so that I was falling.' This refers to this long-extended Edomitic *gâlûth,* and is meant to express: 'I have experienced no push which brought me nearer to falling and complete annihilation than the banishment into the terrible Roman misery.' " It is scarcely to be wondered at that the whole *corpus* of rabbinic and medieval literature is filled with passionate indictments of "infamous Edom" and the "blasphemous Roman Empire." Eisenmenger had no difficulty filling several hundred pages in the second volume of his *Judaism Revealed* with such hostile extracts from rabbinic literature. Neither he nor his anti-Semitic predecessors and successors tried to read these texts against their background in Israel's *Heilsgeschichte.* Had they done so, they would never have arrived at such fantastic conclusions, especially in regard to Jewish ethical precepts, the meaning of which Eisenmenger, beyond doubt, deliberately falsified. Had they tried, the firm axiom of Jewish historical consciousness, sustained in spite of every indignation, would never have been able to escape them: the miseries of

the *gâlûth* are the result of sins, and are, therefore, an exalted expression of God's retributive justice. Indeed, the Jews
—in this respect, also, in contrast to the nations of the world—
even went so far as to create theories which would justify
their persecutors. Thus we have the following exposition of
Genesis 27:40, by R. Jose ben Ḥalafta (Tanna of the fourth
generation, about 160): "When you (*sc.* Edom) see that
your brother [Israel] is shaking off the yoke of the Torah,
then inflict religious persecution upon him and exercise dominion over him." (Bereshit Rabbah 67) However little right
Edom has, on its own account, to engage in wanton violence
and oppression, yet it is justified before God; however great
are the injustices which Israel must suffer in the *gâlûth,* the
injustice itself is the judgment of God. That is the true Jewish philosophy of history!

But exile and suffering, the means of propitiation granted
to the Israelites (Sanh. 37b), are, of course, not the final word
of God. Confidence in ultimate deliverance never vanished.
The greater the suffering, the stronger became the messianic
expectation: "The Israelites spoke before the Holy One,
blessed be his name: 'Lord of the universe, thy foes have indeed placed a heavy yoke upon our necks; but we know that
one day they shall be destroyed, as it is written in Psalm
92:10: "For, lo, thine enemies shall perish; all the workers
of iniquity shall be scattered."'" (Midrash, *loc. cit.*) In the
Eighteen Benedictions the coming of the time is solemnly
implored in which God will destroy the *memsheleth sâdôn*
(rule of evil) from the earth. But deliverance does not come
because it is merited. Some see a connection with *teshûbhâh*
(repentance, return); many others see it as unmotivated as
the original election itself. Midrash Tehillim on 107:1 says:
"Not because of your righteousness or the uprightness of your
hearts are you going in to possess the land (Deut. 9:5).

Neither have I done this for the sake of Abraham, Isaac, and Jacob. Why, then? For the sake of my great name. David said, 'Since he does it for the sake of his great name, give thanks unto the Lord, for he is good.' " It is not the Messiah, that is, a human instrument of God's will, that brings deliverance. Instead, continues the Midrash, explaining Isaiah 35:10, "the ransomed of the Lord shall return. That is, not those delivered by Elijah, nor those delivered by the royal Messiah, but those delivered by God." If up to the present day, God has not yet brought about deliverance, it is because of perseverance in sin. Would all Israel repent for only one day (Exod. Rabbah 25, at 16:29), or would Israel celebrate only one Sabbath as the law requires (Mid. on Ps. 95:7)—so teaches the Amora Rabbi Levi—the Messiah would be already at hand. For this reason, J. T. Yoma I, 1 concludes that "every generation in whose days the sanctuary is not rebuilt is to be viewed as though the sanctuary were destroyed in their days."

The so-called "classical" passage of post-Biblical messianic literature, frequently referred to by eschatological writings, is found in Sanhedrin 97-98. The majority of the scholars whose views are expressed there come from the last generation of the Tannaim; as contemporaries to the event, they still retained a painful memory of the defeat of Bar Kokhba's insurrection, together with the realistic expectation of a political Messiah.[31] They expressed the conviction that the future course of secular history would not consist of an increase in happiness and devotion, but in suffering and enmity toward God, until in reality "the time is fulfilled"; i.e., the commencement of the Messianic Age. Mishnah Soṭah IX, 14, which should be cited at this point, gives a definite theory of stages in the historical decline. *When* this will happen, no one knows—for which reason, all attempts to calculate the time have been forbidden—because no man can view the history of the world through the eyes of God. But for Jews of all periods, the expectation of the Messiah has remained an expectation of the *future*.

This has been Israel's reply to the Church throughout the centuries: deliverance is not yet here; it is yet to come. It can come tomorrow. The *gâlûth* is present, but *ge'ullâh* (deliverance) is always imminent. The seventh of the Eighteen Benedictions reads: "Look upon our misery and take up our cause. And deliver us speedily for thy name's sake, for thou art a strong deliverer. Blessed art thou, O God, deliverer of Israel." And again: "Blow upon the shofar for our redemption; lift high the banner to collect our scattered people, and summon us together from the four corners of the earth. Blessed art thou, O God, who gatherest the dispersed of thy people Israel." In order to underline the fact that the Messiah has not yet come, but that we await him *kol yôm* (every day), there was added a special benediction to the Eighteen, probably to combat the claims of Christianity: *eth ṣemaḥ Dâwîdh* (the sprout of David). (Cf. Elie Munk: *Die Welt der Gebete, Kommentar,* Frankfurt, 1933, Vol. I, pp. 184 f.)

The Church teaches that the content of the New Covenant is Jesus' suffering and death for the Gentile world. In most cases, the Jews have left this an open question and have said nothing about it; ultimately, it was beyond their ability to discuss. But for those who deserted Judaism for the Church, the *meshummâdhîm,* the Tannaim in the age of Gamaliel II, the first patriarch and president of the Sanhedrin at Jamnia, inserted into the Eighteen Benedictions the Birkat ha-Minim, the prayer for the defeat of slanderers and the extirpation of mischief-makers: "May the *noṣrîm* [Jewish Christians] and the *mînîm* [other Jewish heretics] perish suddenly, may they be blotted out of the book of life, not to be recorded there together with the righteous." (Thus in the original recension of the Eighteen Benedictions according to the Palestinian rite; cf. Elbogen, *op. cit.;* 36 JQR, 1897, pp. 154 f.; and elsewhere.) If God is the God of truth, there can be for Jews no salvation other than within the law of the *berîth,* the covenant which God concluded with the fathers, which cannot be revoked or annulled. Contrary to his own theory, Paul himself is forced to admit this (Rom. 11:29): "For the gifts and the call of God are irrevocable." Therefore, this covenant could not be done away with, either through the appearance of Christ or through the destruction of the temple; it is a covenant for *all ages,* as God himself declares upon Sinaï (Deut. 29:13-14), and confirms through the mouth of the prophet: "Thus saith the Lord, Who giveth the sun for a light by day, and the ordinances of the moon and of the stars for a light by night, Who stirreth up the sea, that the waves thereof roar, the Lord of hosts is His name: If these ordinances depart from before Me, saith the Lord, then the seed of Israel also shall cease from being a nation before Me for ever." (Jer. 31:35-36)

4 LAW VERSUS FAITH

All the Christian objections we have raised up to this point and the corresponding Jewish replies pale into insignificance before the *fourth* point of dispute, the one which was decisive in the life of Saul of Tarsus: whether the law has not found its fulfillment and been abolished through belief in the "Lord and Saviour, Jesus of Nazareth."[32] The conflict between Israel and the Church has been carried on for nineteen hundred years with the statement of Pauline theology that this is the case. From the Christian point of view, this has been well justified, since the decision must ultimately be

made, and the truth decided, upon the basis of this question
—at least the truth which God has granted Israel and which
he has granted Christianity. Wherever in the narrow con-
fines of history the claims of both these partakers in the
truth have come into collision with each other, there has
been no compromise; nor can there ever be.

What is the actual point of the Pauline view, the Christian evaluation of the law? Seen from a vantage point within
Judaism, it is a misconception of monstrous proportions; for
all Christian polemic—and especially modern Protestant
polemic against the law—misconstrues the law of the Jews
as a means of attaining justification in the sight of God (so-
called "justification by works"). Wherever Protestant theologians today seek to use Luther's language, they take over
his point of view, which often simplifies far too much. The
righteous demands of God's law, which in reality is intended
to confirm the covenant, are unintentionally put on the same
footing as the actual "justification by works" of the medieval
Catholic Church, at least in its degenerate form. And all this
because, after his experience on the road to Damascus, Paul
was no longer able to understand what he, as a scholar, had
surely known previously: that the law of the Torah was
given, not to make the Jews righteous and acceptable before
their Father in Heaven, but precisely because it proclaims
the holy *will* of their Father in Heaven. Admittedly, from this
Christian point of view, this took place by divine "necessity."
The rabbinic praises of the law can be understood only in
this sense of fulfilling God's will, and never in the sense of
some ethics of merit, no matter how fashioned. As an example of this praise, we shall cite the characteristic statement
of R. Eliezer ben Jacob: "Whoever carries out a commandment gains for himself an advocate; whoever commits a
transgression gains for himself an accuser. Repentance and

good deeds are a shield against the judgment." (Pirke Abot IV, 13) When, in Romans 3:20, Paul says that through works of the law no flesh will be accounted righteous before God, he may well be conducting a justifiable polemic against the erroneous opinions of this or that scholar among his Pharisaic opponents. But he is not saying anything contrary to Holy Scripture, which no more teaches that the law gives justifying merit than that, as Paul has said, "through the law comes knowledge of sin." The Jews of Paul's century knew this as well as those of all centuries. Man falls into sin because he falls short of the revealed will of God. But they did not allow the living experience which confronted them in everyday life to petrify into an a priori law, content in resignation to abrogate the law because of an awareness from the start that it cannot be fulfilled. Now surely Paul's motive is not resignation, but, rather, very conscious reflection, so that he subsequently interprets the function and role of the law on the basis of his faith that he is reconciled with God through the atoning death of Christ—and his interpretation is something *new*. For the law of the covenant is by no means intended to reconcile anyone with God; God himself is the one who reconciles. It is to effect a *union* with God by sanctifying Israel, for God stands in a covenant relationship with Israel by virtue of his free will, his revelation, and his promise.[33] Thus the Midrash has God say to Israel, "Be ye distinguished by the commandments, that ye may be distinguished unto me." (Sifre 75b) The "yoke of the law" and the "yoke of the kingdom of heaven" are thus one and the same yoke. As Hermann Cohen has stated in an important passage from his *Religion der Vernunft aus den Quellen des Judentums,* the law is the "necessary form for fulfilling the *correlation* between God and man." (P. 394)

Paul writes to the Galatians: "Yet who know that a man

is not justified by works of the law but through faith in
Jesus Christ, even we have believed in Christ Jesus, in order
to be justified by faith in Christ, and not by works of the
law, because by works of the law shall no one be justified."
(2:16) If a discussion on this point had ensued, the rabbinic
reply would have been along these lines: What is important
is not "works" of the law or "justification"—only God is
just—but the will of God, which is that Israel be sanctified
through the law proclaimed by him, as it is written, "And
ye shall be holy men unto Me." (Exod. 22:30) This was explained as follows by Rabbi Ishma'el in the Mekiltah on the
passage: "If ye are holy, behold, ye belong to me." And, interpreting the same passage, R. Ise ben Judah, likewise a
Tanna of the second century, says: "If God gives a new law
for Israel, he adds holiness." (Similar statements also by R.
Ḥananiah ben 'Aḳashiah, in M. Makkot III, 16) In order to
prevent misunderstanding, we must also include the interpretation of this passage given by R. Simeon ben Laḳish, in
which God himself is seen to interpret Exodus 22:30: "Thou
wilt think that thou canst become holy, like unto me. But I
alone am holy." (Lev. Rabbah 24, 9, and parallels) In regard
to the Jews' "boasting" in their good works (Rom. 2:23, and
elsewhere), we read in Pesiḳta 98b: "Even when we behold
our good works, we are ashamed because of their insignificance beside God's benefits to us." Or Pesaḥim 118b: "The
congregation of Israel spoke before the Holy One, blessed be
his name: Lord of the universe, though I am poor in meritorious acts, yet nonetheless I belong to thee, and it is within thy
power to help me." There is a famous passage in the Pirḳe
Abot, which we mention only parenthetically, in which the
question whether or not Judaism teaches the merit of works
as the purpose of the law is considered: "Be not like servants
who serve their Lord in order to obtain reward, but be like

servants who serve their Lord *without* intending to obtain a reward. Let only the fear of God be upon you." (I, 3)[34] In Romans 7:18 f., Paul says, "I can will what is right, but I cannot do it. For I do not do the good I want, but the evil I do not want is what I do." The rabbinic reply can only be that this is man's unwillingness to give God the glory, for in his Torah it is written, "This commandment which I command thee this day, it is not too hard for thee, neither is it far off. It is not in heaven, that thou shouldest say: 'Who shall go up for us to heaven, and bring it unto us, and make us to hear it, that we may do it?' Neither is it beyond the sea, that thou shouldest say: 'Who shall go over the sea for us, and bring it unto us, and make us to hear it, that we may do it?' But the word is very nigh unto thee, in thy mouth, and in thy heart, that thou mayest do it." (Deut. 30:11-14)[35] In answer, Paul replies: "For I delight in the law of God, in my inmost self, but I see in my members another law at war with the law of my mind and making me captive to the law of sin which dwells in my members." (Rom. 7:22-23) In the situation of a debate, the rabbinic answer would surely have been a reference to Genesis 4:7: "'. . . sin coucheth at the door; and unto thee is its desire, but thou mayest rule over it.'"

The Pauline doctrinal series is thus complete: the inability of man to keep the law, the assertion that the law is intended to make sin evident, that, as "pedagogue toward Christ," it stimulates sin, until the righteousness demanded by the law, which sin destroyed in the flesh, is fulfilled through the law of Spirit, who gives life in Christ. (Rom. 8:2 ff.) All ages have rightly viewed this doctrine as the principal point of Pauline theology, that in which it goes far beyond the Old Testament. It is quite as un-Jewish as any doctrine of original sin, which denies the freedom of God's creation; nor any doctrine of a Son of God; nor any doctrine of a Trinity, having its historical religious analogies in ancient Egypt (in the triad of Osiris, Isis, Horus), in the Phrygian-Attis-cult and the Syrian-Adonis-cult, or in the Hellenistic Diaspora, rather than in ancient Israel.[36] The Apostle's natal city, Tarsus, was a center of Oriental mystery religions. The Mithra-cult, especially, with its highly developed mysticism of death and resurrection, flourished there. Indeed, Paul's view of the law could in no wise be founded upon Scripture. He denied the power of the law to mediate grace, stating further (according to Gal. 3:19 ff.) that it had been given through the mediation of angels. In this, he joined battle with the Jewish following of the law, a battle which—within the Church's frame of reference—was completely "right," given the faith-experience of salvation in Christ, and "necessary," given his apostolic mission to the Gentile world. It overlooked, however, the *essence* of Judaism. According to the account in Acts 18:5 ff., it was for this reason that he soon ceased—as appears equally "necessary" to the *Jewish* observer—to preach salvation in Christ to the Jews first.[37]

In this conflict over the "law," the Jew is simply not able to enter into the Pauline hypothesis, because, as the essence of Christianity, it lies outside all Jewish possibilities: "Therefore, if any one is in Christ, he is a new creation." (II Cor. 5:17) Judaism was unable to believe Paul's statement that its expected Messiah had already come in the historical Jesus, for the promises coupled with his appearance had not been fulfilled. For the "nations of the world," the beginning of the new aeon and redemption in Christ have, through faith, their historically demonstrable truth. For Israel, on the contrary, this beginning was in the exodus out of Egypt. The death of the "Saviour" on the cross, as a world event, is an "ambiguous phenomenon" (R. Bultmann, *Glaube und Verstehen,* 1933, p. 208), in which more than one *skandalon* is visible to the eye of faith alone. For this reason, "such faith itself belongs to the process of salvation, is itself revelation." (*Loc. cit.,* p. 212) Contemporary Judaism did not encounter the event with this faith; nor, as Judaism, did it consider it necessary to give its good reasons for this, because they correspond to the promises of God. Only subsequent historical circumstances caused individual Jews (cf. the following chapters) to undertake this, and even today, Judaism has not altered the standpoint of its fathers. At the most (cf. chapter V), it can see itself prepared to *acknowledge* that, in an historical event external to itself, something took place in the Gentile world which proceeded from God and was directed toward God, something which assumed and assumes visible form in the Christian Churches. It can do so, obviously, only while contesting any possible relevance which this event might have.

Historically speaking, Paul's missionary activity among the Gentiles laid the groundwork, not for a "Church of Jews and Gentiles,"[38] but for a Church for Gentiles, which emerges out of Judaism. Concerning this activity the Jewish religious historian must still make an observation which concerns not the Christian faith, but the historical events of the time. It was only Paul's missionary work among the Gentiles which wholly brought to light the *practical* consequences of the Pauline denial of the saving power of the law in favor of faith in Jesus the "Christ" as the *mediator* between God and man. As a result of this faith, Paul, the allegorizing midrashist, could set aside the entire ritual and ceremonial law which had made conversion to Judaism unacceptable to the educated Greeks and Romans of the period. This was especially true, since the new religion he preached, with its belief in a Son of God and the atoning power of his sacrificial death, found an easy tie-in with concepts cultivated and spread by the contemporary mystery cults. This had been quite impossible in the case of the Mosaic law and its ethical rigorism. In regard to circumcision, the Apostle writes to the Galatians: "Now I, Paul, say to you that if you receive circumcision, Christ will be of no advantage to you. . . . You are severed from Christ, you who would be justified by the law; you have fallen away from grace." (Gal. 5:2-4) "For neither circumcision counts for anything, nor uncircumcision, but a new creation." (*Ibid.,* 6:15) And just as Paul and emergent Christianity spiritualized the circumcision of the flesh—the outward sign of the Jewish covenant—into a circumcision of the heart (Rom. 2:28-29), in which process the warnings and demands of the prophets were introduced as though proofs of this interpretation, so also the strictness of the Sabbath law (Col. 2:16-17) and the obligatory character of the dietary laws (*ibid.,* 2:17) were surrendered by the nascent Church. Especially in the Epistle to the Hebrews, the cultic prescriptions for sacrifice were reinterpreted allegorically and typologically. The Passover lamb and the sin-offering of the Day of Atonement were referred to Jesus, who, through his sacrificial death, had created for the world an eternal Day of Atonement. All was made to refer to the Church's sacrament of the Lord's Supper (I Cor. 10:16; John 6:53; and elsewhere), which, after a mystical fashion, made the believer a member of the body of Christ.

The Jewish rabbinic schools took positions against all these reinterpretations by denying in principle the legitimacy of allegorical interpretation of Scripture, at least insofar as it resulted in the abrogation of the laws of the Torah. Thus in regard to the literal nature of the law of circumcision, Rabbi Akiba teaches: The commandment "be thou whole-hearted" (Gen. 17:1) was a sign to Abraham to teach him the manner of circumcision, that it refers neither to the foreskin of the ear

(Jer. 6:10), nor to the circumcision of the lips (Exod. 6:30), nor yet to that of the heart (Jer. 9:26), that is, it is not to be interpreted allegorically. Rather, in Genesis 17:1 the foreskin of the body is specifically intended. (Bereshit Rabbah, 46) In spite of this, there are those who teach this doctrine—the nonobligatory nature of circumcision, the Sabbath, the feasts—and blaspheme against Scripture by reinterpreting it. Concerning them, Pirke Abot III, 15 (and in a similar vein also Mish. Sanh. XI, 1) declares as follows: Whoever desecrates what has been sanctified [the Sabbath], whoever profanes the feasts, whoever publicly causes the face of his neighbor to pale, whoever destroys the covenant of our father Abraham, and whoever interprets the law falsely, though he possess knowledge of the Torah and do good deeds, he has no share in the world to come.[39] Those who are antinomians by principle and all who disdain the law presume "to uproot something which is for Israel a fence against sin." (J.T. Ber. 6a) In order to counter antinomianism of the Pauline stamp, which wished merely to retain the decalogue as a moral code while discarding the rest of the law (basing itself on Matt. 19:16-19 and parallels), the daily recitation of the decalogue was banished from public worship during the time of Rabbi Gamaliel II, that is, under the reign of Domitian. This was clearly done in order to combat this particular false doctrine. At the same time, the *Birkat ha-Minim* was introduced. (On these correlations, see Aptowitzer, *MGWJ* 74, pp. 104 ff.)

Paul claimed that the New Covenant had abrogated the law, that in place of the law a new revelation had taken place. The Jews replied: "It is written in Deuteronomy 30: 11-12, 'This commandment is not in heaven,' therefore do not say that there has arisen another Moses, who brought another Torah from heaven. I testify to you that nothing of

the Torah remained in heaven." (Debarim Rabbah, VIII)[40]
This was quite evidently intended as a reply to the Christians
and to all who thought a supplement to the Torah possible,
or believed in a new revelation yet to come.

It now remains to observe what portion of the Pauline opposition between law and faith has been preserved to the
present day in popular theology. The Old Testament is
thought to proclaim the law, while the New proclaims faith.
In the process, an intermediate position, already almost half
way to the New Covenant, is occupied by the guardians of
Israel's covenant, the prophets, whose function is seen as being to look forward to Christ and on the basis of him to
criticize the actions of their contemporaries. In reality, there
is a further circumstance; in addition to the fact that reverent
obedience to the eternal will declared through law stands at
the center of the Torah, while faith, in a divine figure (the
Son or the incarnate Word), stands at the center of the Gospel. Almost as though to make up for his desubstantiation of
the law of circumcision, the dietary regulations, the Sabbath
regulations, and the rules for the feasts, Paul extends *backward* the principle of the New Covenant, faith in Christ
Jesus. According to Paul, Jesus was to set aside the law even
among the Jews, setting in its place a relationship with God.
This relationship was to be the fundamental principle of all
historical events even prior to the new revelation. Besides
Galatians 3, our primary reference is to the eleventh and
twelfth chapters of the Epistle to the Hebrews, where Abel,
Enoch, Abraham, Isaac, Jacob, Joseph, Moses, Gideon, Sam-
son, Samuel, David, and the prophets "through faith con-
quered kingdoms, enforced justice, received promises," and so
forth. They all, "well attested by their faith," are "a cloud of
witnesses" to "Jesus, the pioneer and perfecter of our faith."
The final claim of the author of the Epistle to the Hebrews

was certainly rejected by the Jews as curious speculation; but they, too, knew equally well how to sing the praises of faith, though for them it was no mysterious gift of grace, but the simple expression of firm trust in God. The Mekiltah on Exodus 14:31 may be cited here as typical of many similar passages: " 'And they believed in the Lord, and in His servant Moses.' Great is the faith with which the Israelites believed in Him Who spoke, and the world was. For as a reward for the Israelites' belief in the Lord, the holy spirit rested upon them. And so you will find that our father Abraham inherited this world and the world to come solely through the merit of his faith, the faith by which he 'believed in the Lord,' as it is written: 'And he believed in the Lord; and He counted it to him for righteousness.' " (Gen. 15:6)[41] R. Nehemiah said: "Everyone who ventures a single word by faith is worthy to have the holy spirit rest upon him. . . . And likewise you will find that our father Abraham inherited this world and the world to come only on the merit of the faith by which he believed in the Lord. And so you will find that the Israelites were delivered out of Egypt only as a reward for their faith, as it is written in Exodus 4:31: 'And the people believed.' " Praises of faith are cited, such as that of Moses in Exodus 17:12 and the faith of the fathers is praised, as in II Chronicles 20:20; Jeremiah 5:3; Isaiah 26:2; Psalms 92:2, 118:20; and so forth.

In summary, then, we must conclude that the contrast between merit earned by works and by faith, righteousness of the law and of the Gospel, prophecy and fulfillment, is just as popular as it is false. It is not here that the contrasts lie. The book that Christians, from their own point of view, call the "Old Testament," itself speaks of faith. But this faith neither foretells Christ Jesus, nor is it in any sense a preparation for him. In all truth it is nothing other than the firm, confident faith of the covenant people in God the creator,

who brought the people out of Egypt, confirmed upon Sinai
the covenant concluded with the fathers, giving it written
confirmation through the revelation of his laws, which the
prophets merely confirmed for the people through renewed
proclamation of the law in periods of apostasy. Scripture
usually calls this faith the fear of God (*yir'ath adhônay,* or
yir'ath shâmayim). It is the fundamental principle of the
"Old Covenant." But this faith must not be played off against
the Patriarchs Abraham, Isaac, and Jacob, as Hebrews 11 beyond doubt tries to do, as though they—already beloved and
elected by God—on account of their faith had no need of the
law, or even stood opposed to the law. In the interest of com-
bating such teachings, we can see the tendency of the Talmud
to have the patriarchs be most strict in keeping all the ritual
and ceremonial laws, together with the even more difficult
rabbinic regulations, saying that although they did not yet
know of them, they foresaw them. As is well known, this goes
so far that not only does Abraham keep the Torah before it
exists (M. Ḳiddushim IV, 14)—according to the Talmudic
way of thinking, how could he otherwise have been the
model of Jewish piety?—e.g., occupying himself with tefillin
and rabbinic regulations (Ber. Rabbah 49; and *passim*), but
God himself learns from his Torah. ('Abodah Zarah 3b; and
passim) All this is certainly not to be taken literally. Those
who taught it in order to combat Christian attacks on the law
were well aware of its allegorical nature. Nevertheless, from
all of it, there speaks that high esteem for the Torah which
was the real Jewish reply to Paul.

Saul of Tarsus was not an epoch-making figure in Israel.
The great majority of the Jews did not undergo baptism
rather than circumcision, but, rather, left it to the Christians
to conquer the world for *their* God, whom even Jesus had
recognized as his Father. Thus Christianity became a world

religion, and the rabbis deliberately drew the "fence about the law," by extending its scope again and again. For the Torah alone and in itself brings salvation to the Jews; it strengthens them in this world, and gives them the promise of the world to come. According to the faith of the Jews during the age of Jesus, it is the *only* way to God. Upon the keeping of it depends God's destiny for this world and the salvation of man for the world to come. Therefore, Midrash Tehillim 17, 7 has God himself speak after this fashion: My Torah is in your hand; your deliverance is in my hand. If you will keep my Torah, I will bring about your deliverance.

For the Jews there can be no other salvation than that which comes from God, in the face of which all hopes coupled to historical events are deceptive. This is the result of Jewish historical experience over thousands of years. R. Johanan bar Nappaḥa (died 279) expressed it similarly in Midrash Tehillim 36, 10, which has meaning for Jews of all succeeding ages: "After the slavery in Egypt came the deliverance through Moses, after the slavery in Babylon came the deliverance through Daniel. Then came the persecutions by Elam, Media, and Persia, and deliverance through Mordecai and Esther. Then slavery under Greece, and deliverance through the Hasmonaeans and their sons. Then they came into the Roman captivity. Then the Israelites said: We are tired of being delivered and subjugated, delivered and again subjugated. We want no more 'deliverance' at the hands of men. *Deliverance* comes only from God."

IV

THE CONTINUATION OF THE DEBATE IN THE MIDDLE AGES

W E CAN hardly expect to make a complete survey of the literature of the age which extended from the completion of the Babylonian Talmud (about 500) to the emancipation of the Jews in Western Europe for this period covers nearly thirteen centuries. The questions we have discussed in the previous chapter were repeatedly taken up afresh, were varied and developed further; but the points of conflict between Christianity and Judaism in these decisive questions remained unchanged. Many traits of apologetic and polemic literature became intensified and clarified as the ultimate form of the Christian Church became visible, and this Church compelled the Jews to allow questions to be put to them concerning their peculiar nature, their origin, and their destiny. In the Middle Ages there developed a literature of systematic apologetic philosophy, today comprehended under the title "medieval Jewish religious philosophy." Between the ninth and the fifteenth centuries, these scholars undertook to express the religious truths of Judaism in the categories and within the conceptual system of their contemporary environment. One day they were defending themselves against the Karaites and the Islamic Mu'tazila, the next against Aristotelian philosophy, and the next against Christian dogmatics. Besides this copious literature standing under the general heading of philosophy,[42] there developed a specialized apologetic literature for everyday use, especially for the occasions of religious disputation, when these occurred. This literature deals with scriptural proofs and refutations, and frequently assumes the nature of polemic.[43] In addition, we have the numerous commentaries, and commentaries upon commentaries, the decisions and replies of the Middle Ages, which contribute to the illumination of specific problems or passages relevant to our theme. All of these would have to be examined and discussed, were a religious scholar ever to undertake, as his life's work, to write a history of the Jewish faith and the understanding of this faith. In this study we can and shall indicate only a few high points in this development, paying special attention to the further development of such arguments as are singled out for special emphasis through the influence of continuous historical suffering. These assume importance in the argument because they define Jewish doctrine more sharply or delimit it properly from the doctrine of Christianity.

1 DEBATES

Let us first of all examine the content of the medieval "religious dialogues" preserved for us in the *Shebaṭ Jehudah* ("The Rod of Judah") of Ibn Verga, (ed. A. Wiener, Hannover, 1856), in the Wagenseilschen collection (*Tela ignea*

Satanae, Altdorf, 1681), and in other sources, where the principal points of contention are discussed.[44] Especially suitable for studying this question are the accounts of the disputations of Paris (1240), Barcelona (1263), and Tortosa (1413-14), each of which had been provoked by Christians.

The Paris disputation falls within the pontificate of Gregory IX. It was convened by the French king, Louis IX, in the presence of the high French clerics and state dignitaries; it lasted three days (June 25-27). An apostate named Donin (with the Christian name Nicolas) had leveled an accusation of thirty-five points against Judaism, especially against the Talmud. The Jewish protagonist, who had to reply to these points, was the Tosafist R. Jeḥiel ben Joseph. The major charges were directed against passages from the Talmud which were said to contain slanders against the person of Jesus and to recommend amoral behavior toward Christians. Other attacks were made upon the Kol Nidre prayer of the Day of Atonement and the Minim prayer of the Eighteen Benedictions. All of these charges could easily be refuted as misinterpretations or deliberate distortions of text or meaning; but this did not prevent twenty-four wagonloads of copies of the Talmud from going up in flames in a public square in Paris.

More significant from the doctrinal point of view was the Disputation of Barcelona, in which the King of Aragon forced Moses Naḥmanides to answer three questions laid before him by his opponent—once against an apostate, Pablo Christiani. These questions went to the root of the conflict: (1) Has the Messiah already appeared, or not? (2) Is the Messiah promised by the prophets a divine or a human figure? (3) Who holds the correct faith, the Christians or the Jews?[45] Naḥmanides' answers are remarkable because they evidence a faith which has been tempered by historical experience. The first question was whether the Messiah had already appeared in Jesus; this hinged upon the exegesis of messianic passages from Scripture. Naḥmanides refuted the Christian contention through quotation of the prophets (Isa. 2:4; Micah 4:3; and *passim*); their promises obviously had not yet been fulfilled, since war and bloodshed, injustice and outrage, still held sway. Indeed, the Christians themselves were the most warlike men of all. Jesus had not freed man from original sin, for the punishments decreed by God (according to Christian doctrine) as a result of the sin of the first man—hard labor for man and pangs of birth for women (Gen. 3:16-19)—continue to remain in force. Naḥmanides answers the second question as follows: In the view of tradition, the Messiah was to be a man of flesh and blood. According to Isaiah 11:1, the Messiah is called a shoot from the stock of Jesse; and although this was true of Jesus with respect to his descent on his mother's side, such maternal inheritance did not enter into consideration for succession to the throne of David. He settles the last question by referring to the unreasonable nature of Christian doctrine. This disputation also ended with the banishment of the Jewish protagonist.

The third disputation was held in Tortosa, before the schismatic Pope Benedict XIII (for further information see *Shebat Jehudah* 40); its equally unfortunate ending helped prepare the way for the castastrophe which was to befall the Jews in Spain. Instead of describing it, we shall refer to the philosophical work, the *'Iḳḳarim* ("The Book of Principles"), of one of the leading Jewish participants, Joseph Albo (died *ca.* 1435).[46] According to its introduction, this was intended to serve as a point of departure for discussions among adherents of various religions; but the list of its arguments, as well as the structure of its philosophical system, rarely has anything new to offer, having more the nature of a thesaurus.

The primary importance of the *'Iḳḳarim* for Jewish religious philosophy rests in the fact that Albo reduced to three the thirteen religious dogmas of Maimonides: God, revelation, and retribution.

To reach his goal—the creation of a basis for doctrinal discussion—Albo proceeds by attempting to create a common basis for all religions by means of a suitable definition of the concept of possible revelation. This procedure leads to a determination of disputed dogmas (*'iḳḳârîm perâṭiyyîm*), and the definition of the discrepancy and aberration of Christian, Karaite, and Mohammedan doctrine from which Albo had postulated the rational idea of revelation at the outset (*'Iḳḳarim* I, 26). According to Albo, the six hundred and thirteen laws which the Talmud (Makkot 24a) derived from the Torah are divine arrangements of sacramental character for the furthering of the good of the human soul (III, 39). The soul, in turn, achieves to differing levels of virtue, depending upon the number of religious duties fulfilled (III, 30-36). Albo interprets the covenants with Adam, Noah, Abraham, and Moses as acts of legislation. He links the question of whether this legislation can be amended to the giving of the law upon Sinai, which took place before a company of six hundred thousand men. This historical foundation for the binding nature of the event is employed universally in medieval disputations. On the basis of the logical structure of his religious system, Albo, *pace* Maimonides, derives the immutability of the law as a corollary of revelation (III, 19); then, borrowing from Simon Duran, but without quoting him, he denies the possibility of a new covenant (in the infamous 25th chapter of the third book, removed by censorship from most editions). He goes on to contest the possibility of the Trinity on exegetical as well as formal-logical grounds;[47] on the basis of the Gospel records, casts doubts upon the Apostles' understanding of and familiarity with the Bible; and finally, impugns the virgin birth and Davidic descent of Jesus, without which any argument over his Messiahship would be a priori settled. With Albo, messianic doctrine undergoes a general weakening; it is no longer a fundamental dogma. Nevertheless, it was he who, at Tortosa, had to give his views on complicated questions dealing with the calculation of the end of time and Jewish messianism (according to Shebeṭ Jehudah 71 and 74). He points out a misreading on the part of St. Jerome in translating Psalm 19:8: In "The law of the Lord is perfect," Jerome translated *temîmâh* incorrectly as "spotless" [*immaculata*], rather than "perfect, complete." He then finishes the chapter with the conclusion that "the law of Moses is exalted above every defect, and partakes of all possible perfection." Further, in agreement with the Yalḳuṭ Shimeoni, at another place he interprets the last verse of Leviticus: "These are the commandments," to mean that henceforth no prophet may introduce any innovation; and the conclusion of this sentence, "which the Lord commanded unto Moses," to be a sealing of the fact that he (Moses) who has been sent, has been worthy of him who sends.

Besides making clear the supernatural character of the Jewish religion, the three dogmas—God, revelation, and retribution—had the apologetic purpose of proving that Christianity was not in agreement with the rational ideas of the "objective" (*n.b.* Jewish) concept of revelation.[48]

2 SAADYAH

In the brief survey presented here, we have observed the development of the method of debate characteristic of medieval religious philosophy in its polemic against Christian doctrine. With this intent, we have examined briefly the contribution of Joseph Albo. We now turn back to the founder of medieval Jewish religious philosophy, Saadyah Gaon (882-942). With his work *Emunot ve-Deot* ("Faith and Knowledge"), it was his task to define the traditional Jewish faith of the tenth century vis-à-vis the Karaite heresy and the Islamic Mu'tazila which dominated its entire environment. We shall then briefly see what light the work of Judah ha-Levi (*ca.* 1075-1141) can shed on our subject, since beyond doubt the high point of medieval Jewish philosophy was reached in the positions taken in his *Kuzari*. By presenting certain typical positions taken by both these thinkers, which were borrowed by others and, in part, developed further,[49] we can save ourselves the task of further exposition for the purpose of orientation.

Saadyah's religio-philosophical position is set down in his major systematic work, *Emunot ve-Deot* (quotations based on the translation published by Jul. Fürst, Leipzig, 1845). It is based on the *mu'tazilitic* thought of the Islamic Kalam, which moved very far in the direction of Jewish thought through its strict interpretation of the concept of the unity of God and its acknowledgment of free will. Through the examination of one central problem, the relationship between reason and revelation, natural knowledge and religious truth, Saadyah presented all subsequent Jewish philosophers with the decisive formulation of the question. The relativistic tendency of modern times, which assumes a multiplicity of revealed religions and hence of modes of participation in the truth, was completely foreign to Saadyah, as it was to all medieval thinkers. For them, the religious truth of Judaism is secured by the exclusive nature of the concept of revelation, the content of which can be understood by reason; it can, in fact, be identified with this revelation. The pedagogical purpose of revelation is to open up truth to all those who are incapable of independent thought. To the philosophers, able to discover the truth for themselves by rational methods, revelation gives a fixed, unshakable foundation as security against all doubt. But if the content of revelation in Judaism is, per se, identical with uncorrupted human reason, all religions differing from the Jewish religion—for Saadyah, this means Christianity and Islam—must be human creations, which falsely ascribe divine origin to themselves. Saadyah continues this line of thought in a detailed critique of the concept of the Trinity, which became standard for the Jewish polemic of the Middle Ages, as well as in a more apologetic presentation of traditional Jewish doctrine, the exclusive nature of which excludes every other revelation.

The Christian derivation of the doctrine of the Trinity from the Old Testament often proceeds violently enough. It is met by Saadyah first (II, 18-22)—for reasons of brevity and clarity, we must unfortunately omit detailed presentation of his chain of reasoning—through an interpretation of the two *positive* moments in the Jewish concept of God. These are life and wisdom, for only as a wise and living being can God carry out the activity of creation. The Christian, on the other hand, differentiates both these attributes from the essence of God, and then differentiates them further into independent substances. (Jesus appearing in the flesh is the life-principle; the Holy Spirit is the wisdom-principle.) Thus Christian theology separates the divine attributes "existent," "living," and "wise" from each other and from the essence of God; this makes God a composite being, that is, corporeal—everything that exhibits differentiation *is* corporeal. Everything corporeal is a creature, first alive, then dead, first wise, then foolish, which cannot be stated of God.

On the contrary, life and wisdom—expressed by God—are emanations from his *power,* upon which, according to Saadyah, the concept of God is based; attributed to man, they are products of an agent different in kind from the human body (*sc.* divine creative power). Since the Christian doctrine of the Trinity seeks to obliterate this basic difference between the creator and the creature (a difference which, by definition, admits no reconciling mediation), Christianity denies the true nature of God.[50] To this logical argument, Saadyah appends (II, 2) a critique and refutation of all attempts to hypostasize the attributes of divine activity through Christological exegesis. In II, 25, he sets forth a polemic against the doctrine of the Logos as the actual basis of Christology. In II, 26, he mentions four different Christian sects which, taken together, represent to him the Christianity of the period, and, therefore, must all be refuted: "Against the monophysites, who taught that the body and spirit of Jesus are from God, Saadyah refers to his arguments against the doctrine of the emanation of the spirit from God. The second sect, the duophysites, are countered by the same argument, and, in addition, by the rebuke that, according to them, the body of Jesus, though an ordinary (not emanated from God) creature, assumed the divine nature. The third sect believed the spirit and body of Jesus were originally ordinary creatures; the previously mentioned argument is brought against them: no creature can assume the divine nature. Against the fourth sect, which acknowledged Jesus merely as a prophet, reference is made to the arguments (yet to be described) against the abrogation of the Torah and against the Messiahship of Jesus—arguments which are directed against all Christian schools of thought."[51] Saadyah's method in the philosophic treatment of this question pointed the way for all later interest in Jewish apologetics and polemic. The train of reasoning in the "refutation" of the doctrine of the Trinity found many adherents among his successors, particularly penetrating being the further work done by Moses ben Salomo.[52]

The third tractate deals with prescriptions and prohibitions. In it, Saadyah enters upon the question whether the law can be abrogated. The purpose, expressed in the second and also at the end of the eighth tractate, is to heap up "proofs toward the refutation of those [*sc.* Christians] who believe an abolishment of the law possible." In III, 16, he writes as follows: "The children of Israel have transmitted a tradition that the prophets said to them that the laws of the Torah would not be abolished." Saadyah then continues by affirming that his understanding of the Scriptures afforded him the following proofs of this view:

1. that with many laws there is written "a perpetual covenant" which shall endure "throughout their generations" (Exod. 31:16)

2. that the Torah itself says: "Moses commanded us a law, An inheritance of the congregation of Jacob" (Deut. 33:4);

3. that our nation, the children of Israel, is now a nation only in its laws; and, since the creator promised (according to Jer. 31:37) that the nation will exist as long as heaven and earth exist, it follows of necessity that the law will exist for the duration of the world.

Saadyah then appends exegeses of II Chronicles 20:17; Jeremiah 31:30-37; Obadiah 1:1; and other passages, disputing the Christian interpretation of them. Here, as a final example, we shall give only his objections to the Christian interpreters of Jeremiah 31:30 ff. (III, 28): "See then what follows, for he has plainly declared that the new covenant is the Torah itself, as it is written, 'I will write my Torah in their inward parts, and in their heart will I write it.' (V, 23) And the difference from the first covenant consists only in the fact that in this age it shall no longer be broken, as happened with the covenant made with the fathers in the exodus from Egypt." (V, 32) Among the further objections and cavils by Christians, which are listed in an appendix to the tractate, the treatment of the eleventh is interesting: How can the divine law be good and true if the nation which confesses it is so mean and contemptible? The answers discussed in the previous chapter also return in the case of Saadyah, but the intensification of the paradoxical factor is perhaps noteworthy: "The Almighty has exalted the nations, and yet they do not believe in him, so that the argument is destroyed; the Israelites he has humbled, and yet they do not renounce his law, so that truth is plainly upon their side. This in answer to those who say that the Jews seek to obtain prosperity and advantage through the law, and that the heathen do not keep the law because they already have prosperity." (III, 44)

3 JUDAH HA-LEVI

The conviction, grounded in faith, that in historical impotence there can be power provided by God, is given an exceptionally formed and plastic expression in crucial portions of the *Kuzari,* a book written about 1140 by the poet and philosopher Judah ha-Levi (quoted here after the translation published by D. Cassel, Leipzig, 1869). Although written in Arabic (the original title being *The Book of the Proof and Argument in Defense of the Slandered Religion*), the *Kuzari* enjoyed such great popularity that it was widely distributed in Hebrew translations among the Jewish communities of Europe. The historical background of the book is furnished by a legendary tale surrounding the conversion of the king of the "Khazars" by a Jewish scholar about the year 770.[53]

Against this historical background, the King of the Khazars, troubled as he is by serious religious questions, undertakes to talk with a philosopher, a Christian, and a Moslem. Having dismissed them, he then enters into dialogue with a Jewish "master" who rehearses with him many points of Jewish doctrine. What is important is not the original treatment of the philosophical problem of knowledge, or the reappearance of arguments previously rehearsed, but the specific foundation of Jewish historical truth upon the supernatural character of Israel's election. In Judah ha-Levi we find a thoroughly worked-out *doctrine of election*,[54] which, beyond doubt, had an enormous historical function in helping the nation bear its exile. Disagreeing with the *Kuzari,* the master argues that the divine spirit, which rested only upon individuals from Adam to Jacob, came down upon the entire people during the wandering in the wilderness, as the "spirit of love, to be their God." (III, 17; I, 95; and *passim*) Since Sinai, all Israel is at the stage of prophecy, and the one God is in substantial union with the one people. Israel is among the nations "as the heart among its members." (II, 36) This is intended not at all metaphorically; for Judah ha-Levi, election is determined by physical descent according to the seed. For only a very particular tribe among the tribes of the earth is elected in all its generations. The sons of Jacob are singled out as "the elect and the heart" of mankind (I, 103). Therefore, to be consistent, ha-Levi must state that he "who wishes to join himself to the way of Israel will indeed receive, together with his posterity, a great share in the presence of God. But, nevertheless, he who enters into our faith is not equal to him who was born within it; for only to those born within it is prophesy granted, while the highest goal of others is that they learn from the prophets—that they become wise and devout, but not prophets." (I, 115) Even apostasy cannot

eradicate the fact of election. "Were any among them disobedient, so were they expelled; but they remained yet members of the election, because such they were by descent and
natural condition, and were also able to beget posterity
worthy of the election." (I, 95) Nevertheless, this election
is not to be construed as a possession—"the excellence of the
Torah is not founded upon Moses, but rather that of Moses
upon the Torah" (I, 56)—but rather it is an obligation to the
Torah. Its basis is the unfathomable action of God toward
Israel. "We have this obligation because he led us out of
Egypt and revealed to us his glory; for we are the treasure
[*seghullâh*] of mankind." (I, 27) The election does not have
its effect as a charismatic substance belonging to the individual Israelite, given to him immediately at birth, but rather
as a physical disposition, a kind of heightened readiness for
the reception of the divine spirit, which allows him to speak
of an "elect of the elect." (II, 44) These are the devout, the
"true Israelites." They share in the perfect presence of God.

Hardly any other thinker took the fact of the election as
a consequence of the covenant so seriously as did Judah ha-
Levi in his *Kuzari*. He sees man as a truly equal partner in the
Covenant. This is the basis of Jewish theology. Of course, the
royal participant in this conversation, as a Gentile, resists,
to the utmost, granting to Israel such a favored position, above
all the rest of mankind. This is so, on the one hand, because
providence is surely extended over all men; on the other, because it is the Jews who are the most oppressed and least
regarded people of the world. The first objection is grounded
on the particularistic character of the Jewish religion. The
suprarationalist ha-Levi answers that the exaltation of Israel
follows from the unfathomable nature of the will of God,
who in freedom has mercy upon whom he will, as is proved
by his shaping and molding of Jewish history since the time

of Abraham, a providential grace which could never be justified by the merit of Israel (I, 80-88, 103; and *passim*). The
other objection, that of simple reason, provides ha-Levi with
an occasion for delving in its full depth into the problem of
the Exile, thereby doubtless expressing the religious conviction of the Jewish people as it lived at that time. First, the
Jewish master refers the inquiring king to the close connection between earthly suffering and shame of Israel and the
glory and fame which it occupies in the eyes of God. Even
Christians and Moslems make analogous statements about the
golden ages of their religions and the most characteristic element in the life of their founders (I, 113). On the contrary, it
is important that the Jew convert forced oppression into oppression accepted freely in order that he might bear it with
humility. "Yea, were we to suffer exile and oppression in the
name of God, as is fitting, then we should be an ornament to
the age, which we endure with the Messiah, and would has-
ten the coming of future deliverance." (I, 115) As far as the
present condition of Israel is concerned—the interim period
between the second and the temple to come—the master explains that Israel today "is a body without head and without
heart. Not even a body, but scattered bones, like the dry bones
which Ezekiel saw. And yet, king of Kuzar, skeletons in
which vital force yet remains, and which once were creatures
with head, heart, spirit, soul, mind, are better than bodies
which are made of stone and chalk, having heads, eyes, ears,
and all their members in which the breath of life has never
dwelt and can never dwell, which are only figures shaped
like men, but are not men." (II, 29-30) These statements are
of exemplary importance for the self-understanding of Exile
(*gâlûth*)-Judaism, and could not be put differently today,
more than eight hundred years later. In this cultic symbolism,
the heart is the temple, in which stood the ark of the cove-

nant; the head is the priests and the prophets, who conveyed the teaching: "But he who preserves us upright in this state, in dispersion and in exile, is the living God." (II, 32) To this, the *Kuzari* answers: "That is true. For it is otherwise inconceivable that a nation could endure such exile without being absorbed into another nation, especially after so long a period," and his Jewish interlocutor summarizes: "But do not think that because I assent to your words, there lies therein an admission that we are a dead cause. On the contrary, we stand yet in union with that divine spirit, through the laws which he set up as a covenant between us and him, e. g., circumcision, of which it is written, 'My covenant shall be in your flesh for an everlasting covenant.' (Gen. 17:13) Further, the Sabbath, of which it is written, 'It is a sign between Me and the children of Israel for ever.' (Exod. 31:17) In addition, there is the covenant with the fathers, the covenant of the Torah, which he concluded with us on Horeb and a second time upon the plains of Moab, together with promises regarding reward and punishment. Thus we are not to be compared to a dead man, but rather to a sick man of whose recovery all the physicians despair, while he himself hopes for healing from a miracle, from a mighty act, as it is written, 'Can these bones live?'" (II, 33)

Having thus pictured the historical condition of the *goy ḳâdhôsh* (holy people) in the period of the Exile, the master continues with a simile: "Israel is among the nations as the heart is among the members, at once the sickest of all and yet the most healthy." (II, 36) The sickest, because it is exposed to all the assaults and batterings of history; the most healthy, because by virtue of the election, it will continue as long as the world endures.

Ha-Levi, at this juncture, places in the forefront of his argument an explanation for the wretchedness and misery of the

Jews which had been proposed as early as the Hasmonean period (and often connected exegetically with Amos 3:2 and Jeremiah 30:11). The fate of punishment and misfortune which overtook the Jews, he affirms, is a token of great grace. Thus it is written in the second book of Maccabees: "In fact, not to let the impious alone for long, but to punish them immediately, is a sign of great kindness. For in the case of the other nations the Lord waits patiently to punish them until they have reached the full measure of their sins; but he does not deal this way with us, in order that he may not take vengeance on us afterward when our sins have reached their height." (*Ibid.,* 6:13-15) Obviously, *this* form of the doctrine of retribution had to be of great importance for Israel's historical self-understanding. (Cf. also Rashi on Exod. 32:34;[55] J. Albo, *'Ikkarim* IV, 38; *Ḥizzuk 'Emunah* I, 22; also numerous Midrashic passages, ancient and recent.) For the light of the Jews "has gone down only in the eyes of those who do not view us with unclouded eyes, who derive evidence for the extinguishing of our light from our oppression, poverty, and dispersion, just as they extract proofs for the existence of light in others from their greatness, their earthly power and dominion over us." (IV, 21) But, in truth, the degradation of the Jewish people is a definite part of God's plan for the world. It can be understood only from the point of view of election; in this sense the commentators explained again and again the Suffering Servant passages from Isaiah. But the destiny of Israel—and this is the mission of the Jews in the world—is comparable to that of a seed: "It is planted in the earth, where it apparently changes and is transformed into earth, water, and mud, and can scarcely be perceived any longer. But it is just this which transforms earth and water into *its* nature, raising them from one level to the other, so that it frees the elements and transforms them into its own shape, then brings forth husk and leaves," and so forth. Thus, also, the teaching of Moses transforms everyone who follows it into its own likeness, even if it is apparently rejected by all. These nations (*sc.* the Christians and Moslems) are the preparation and introduction for the awaited Messiah. He is the fruit, and his fruit shall they all be, if they acknowledge him; and all shall be *one* tree. Then shall they honor and revere the roots which previously they despised, as we have explained in regard to "Behold, My servant shall prosper." (Isa. 52:13; IV, 23)[56] This conception of Israel's mission and the significance of Christianity and Islam (which were invariably viewed as false doctrines distorting divine truth) led to doctrinal consequences only in a transformed intellectual milieu, long after the close of the Middle Ages, when Salomon Formstecher (cf. Chapter VI), using the foundations of German Idealism, undertook to construct a Jewish theology of history.

4 ISAAC TROKI

Here, at the close of the chapter on the medieval development of the conflict between the faiths, we shall outline the contents of a piece of literature belonging to the controversy, which served exclusively apologetic and polemic purposes. To an extent it can be viewed as typical of this genre, containing the prevailing points of dispute and method of argumentation. For this purpose, we have selected a very late document, in which, without unusually great originality, the author took the results achieved by the medieval commentators who contested Christian exegesis and misinterpretation, together with the polemic material against Christian doctrines available from previous works, and developed them in a way which corresponded to the Jewish religious convictions of the age. We have given preference to the work of the Karaite Isaac ben Abraham Troki (1533?-1594?), *Hizzuk Emunah (Strengthening of the Faith)*, rather than that of R. Yomtob Lipmann Mühlhausen, *Nissahon*, which is occasionally intemperate in its polemic.[57] *Hizzuk Emunah* (cited according to the edition of D. Deutsch, Leipzig, 1873) appeared in 1593, and soon achieved wide circulation, passing through many editions and translations. In the Wagenseil edition, for example, it furnished Voltaire with a mine of anti-Christian arguments (cf. *Melanges* III, p. 344). Until the nineteenth century, it was almost always thought to be the work of a rabbinic Jew.

Hizzuk Emunah is the work of a lifetime. It is, according to a statement in the foreword, a compilation of all the arguments which Isaac Troki had presented against the doctrines of Christianity in numerous disputations. In these he appears for the most part to have encountered Polish anti-Trinitarians belonging to the Socinian movement (the chief witnesses of his polemic are Nicholas Paruta, Martin Czechowitz, and particularly the Polish Bible translator Simon Budny); that is, Christians already having judaizing tendencies. But he also draws into his debates Lutherans, Roman Catholics, and Greek Orthodox; only Calvinists are missing.[58] As a Karaite, he does not need to justify Talmudic expressions and ideas; his strictly biblical orientation makes the Jewish position much easier. His apologetic efforts are primarily centered about the invalidation of Christological interpretation of passages of Scripture by means of exegesis conformed to the text (i.e., not through the glasses of tradition, but with the sight of one's own eyes). Such an approach went hand in hand with demonstration of the absolute authority of the Bible, which required no supplementation.

Finally, the wretched historical condition of the Jews was explained on the basis of the promises and threats of punishment contained in the Scriptures. The polemic of the second portion of *Hizzuk Emunah* attempts to forge weapons against Christian doctrine out of the internal contradictions within the Gospel itself, as well as its contrasts to the statements of the prophets.

In each of the areas of inquiry which Troki pursues, we can cite but one of many which will serve to indicate the method and content of Troki's exposition.

Troki's polemic against scriptural exegesis in support of Christian doctrine, is well illustrated in his explanation of the threat of punishment in paradise (Gen. 2:17), from which was derived the Christian doctrine of original sin. By citing numerous parallel passages also dealing with the punitive consequences of transgressing divine commands, he shows that the passage in question is to be understood literally, and does not contain a second, hidden, sense. The only matter of concern is that eating from the tree of knowledge will entail physical death as a punitive consequence. Numerous passages from the prophets, such as Ezekiel 18:14-32, prove the responsibility of man for his own sins, "that the devout and holy fathers in no case went to Hell and suffered punishment of their souls as a result of Adam's fall. Unlike him, they had not acted contrary to the will of God, but, rather, they found favor in the eyes of the Lord. Eternal salvation was granted them through their own merit, without the necessity for utilizing the merit of others for this salvation, as the Christians arbitrarily fabricate." The same thing is said in Ezekiel 18:20: "The soul that sinneth, it shall die; the son shall not bear the iniquity of the father with him, neither shall the father bear the iniquity of the son with him"; that is, the soul encounters death only as the result of its own sin, not as the result of the sins of others, as is clearly set forth by the words of the prophet. (I, 11)

Isaac Troki's Karaite method has presumably become clear. It was to elucidate passages of Scripture which, to the Jewish way of thinking, are misinterpreted by bringing to bear other passages from the Bible. A further example: Concerning the Torah, the Christians object that the law of Moses is not an eternal, but only a temporary, law. It was in force until the appearance of Jesus; he, however, abolished it, the more so because it was impossible to keep, and brought a new law: the law of love. Troki's answer is that the Gospel itself (Matt. 5:17 ff.) gives the lie to this idea (I, 19). Jesus gave explicit command to keep the law; both he and his disciples were circumcised. According to Acts 16:3, Paul himself circumcised his disciple Timothy; the early Christians still observed the Sabbath, and so forth.

It seems much more as though it were the sum purpose of Christians to do away with the law of our teacher Moses by their own arbitrary power, since neither Jesus nor the Apostles so commanded. Indeed, had Jesus freed them from all the commandments listed in the law of Moses, as they make out, why did he expressly command that a portion be observed, such as, for example, the honoring of father and mother, the love of one's neighbor, meekness, as well as the commandments to abstain from murder, adultery, theft, and false witness?—according to Matthew 19:17 ff. Further, why did the Apostles (according to Acts 15:20 ff.) forbid idolatry, unchastity, the enjoyment of blood, and what is strangled? Moreover, the statement that the Mosaic law has been abolished because it contains penalties of death, while the law of Jesus is a law of love, may be questioned, since Paul, for example, in I Corinthians 5:1, commanded the death of the man who was living with his father's wife. They state further that the law of Jesus is easy to keep, while that of Moses, on the contrary, with all its commandments, is difficult to keep. This likewise does not correspond with reality. In Matthew 19:21, we read that Jesus said to one of his disciples, "If you would be perfect, go, sell what you possess and give to the poor." A similar statement is found in Luke 18:22. It follows from this that the law of Jesus commands one to sell all the goods one possesses and give to the poor, while the Mosaic law commands only that the tenth part of the harvest be given away. (I, 19)

This is a reflection on the question of whether the law of Moses is more difficult to keep than that of Jesus. Troki inquires further why the Christians, if they have already been freed from the Mosaic law, still retain a portion of the prohibited degrees of consanguinity, why Jesus did not give a new law for the conduct of justice among men, and so forth. He could not do so at all, for the Torah is the law of God, and, as such, is immutable, incapable of being supplemented, absolutely perfect, as Deuteronomy 4:2, 13:1, Psalm 19:8-10, and numerous other passages prove. The final prophecy from the mouth of God by the last prophet, "Remember ye the law of Moses My servant, Which I commanded unto him in Horeb for all Israel, Even statutes and ordinances," (Mal. 3:22) likewise proclaims that there shall never be another law than that given to Moses upon Sinai. Even his principal witness, Budny, must admit that the divine law of Moses is perfect and eternal, and except for it there is no divine law, and that "those who assert that there are two laws, that of Moses and that of Jesus, are in error, since Jesus gave no law, but rather commanded that the law of Moses be observed." (I, 20)

After these examples of Troki's legal thinking and his refutation of antinomian arguments, we shall mention briefly his answers to the historical arguments so popular at that time. These are usually quite skillful and more effective. A Christian scholar asks whether the prophetic promises were not already fulfilled at the time of the second temple, and why the Roman *gâlûth* has lasted so long in comparison to earlier exiles. Troki gives the following answers: The words of the prophets were fulfilled only partially by the previous exiles (the seventy years of the Babylonian exile were intended only to let the soil rest and make good the neglected sabbatical years), the time of deliverance has not yet come, only this fourth "present, long-enduring, oppressive, and wretched *gâlûth*" can efface our sinfulness and uncleanness, so that hereafter we shall have to endure no more *gâlûth*, as it is written in Lamentations 4:22: "The punishment of thine iniquity is accomplished, O daughter of Zion, He will no more carry thee away into captivity." Further, we read in Amos 1:6, "Thus saith the Lord: For three transgressions of Gaza, Yea, for four, I will not reverse it: Because they carried away captive a whole captivity, To deliver them up to Edom." This fourth *gâlûth* lasts so long only "because of the multitude of our sins, misdeeds, and transgressions." The appearance of salvation depends upon our improvement, for which reason the date of the end is kept secret by God, as it is written in Deuteronomy 32:34, " 'Is not this laid up in store with Me, Sealed up in My treasuries?'" Edom and Ishmael have still not been destroyed; even the much controverted dates of Daniel remain hidden and mysterious. Though the Jews have now languished in the *gâlûth* for more than fifteen hundred years, this proves nothing; for between the creation and the flight out of Egypt, 2,448 years passed. As Isaac Arama ('Akedat Yiṣḥak on Parashat Waethanan) and Isaac Abrabanel also teach: If the Messiah needed many millennia to free the souls of the devout of most ancient time from the power of Satan, why does the Christian find it difficult to believe that God will also rescue evil from this present exile, of which perhaps only half has passed?

(End of I, 8) Even the Kingdom proclaimed by the Christian faith has by no means concerned, for the faith of Mohammed still rules half the earth. (End of I, 5)

Next, Troki collects all the signs of the onset of the messianic age, which were accepted by rabbinic and Karaite Jews from the Middle Ages down to the emancipation. Given the expectation of these signs, derived from prophecies literally understood, Jesus' messiahship could not be taken seriously. These are the following predictions of the prophets, still unfulfilled: (1) the gathering of the ten tribes under a Davidic king (Ezek. 37:21-22); (2) the battle between Gog and Magog (Ezek. 38 and 39); (3) the cleaving of the Mount of Olives (Zech. 14:4); (4) the drying up of the river in Egypt at the time of gathering of the dispersed (Isa. 11:15); (5) the issuing of living water from the site of the temple in Jerusalem (Ezek. 47:1 ff.); (6) ... ten men from other nations take hold of the hem of a Jew's coat and say to him: "We will go with you, for we have heard that God is with you" (Zech. 8:23); (7) the going up of the remnant of the nations to Jerusalem for worship (Zech. 14:16); (8) the appearance there of the nations on sabbaths and new moons (end of Isaiah); (9) the expulsion from the land of idols and false prophets and unclean spirits (Zech. 13:2; Isa. 42:17); (10) in the whole world there shall be but one faith, that of Israel (Isa. 52:1, 60:1 ff.; and *passim*); (11) in the whole world there shall be but one kingdom, the kingdom of the Israelites as God's saints (Num. 24:17; Isa. 60:10-12; Dan. 7:27; and *passim*); (12) eternal peace (Isa. 2:4; Micah 4:3; and *passim*); (13) peace between the wild beasts and domestic animals (Isa. 11:6-9); (14) the final end of sin (Ezek. 36:33-37, 37:23-24; Zeph. 3:13; and *passim*); (15) the end of suffering (Isa. 65:19 ff.); (16) renewal of the covenant as sanctification for the Israelites (Ezek. 37:26-28; Jer. 31:34 ff.;

and *passim*); (17) the arrival of Elijah (Mal. 4:5); (18) the building of the future temple (Ezek. 40-46); (19) the division of the land according to the twelve tribes (Ezek. 47:13 ff.); (20) the resurrection of the dead (Isa. 26:19; Dan. 12:2; and *passim*). "Beyond doubt these and similar prophecies have not yet been fulfilled, and of necessity must yet be fulfilled; for God is not a man, that he should lie. Therefore, they all together bear witness that the Messiah promised by the prophets—blessed be their memory—whose arrival we await has not yet come." (I, 6)

From this scriptural denial of any possibility of Jesus' messiahship, Isaac Troki passes in the second portion of his work to an attack on the credibility of the Gospels.[59] Almost two hundred years previously, Simon Buran, in his *Kelimmat ha-Goyim* (The Reproach of the Nations), had performed the exegetical preparation for all who were to follow: Mark and Luke did not write their accounts as eyewitnesses. Their works suffer from internal contradictions and betray faulty knowledge of the Bible; events are represented tendentiously, in order to support *ex post facto* the messiahship of Jesus. For example, John the Baptist is designated as Elijah, since he must precede the Messiah, according to the belief of the period; John, finally, under direct questioning, denies such an identity (John 1:21). Or, the Messiah must be a son of David, and, therefore, subsequently, Matthew and Luke constructed two Davidic genealogies. Since this genealogy is also proved for Joseph, the evangelists unintentionally admitted the natural human birth of Jesus. Mary's virginity before and after the birth is to be viewed as a false midrashic interpretation of Isaiah 66:7. According to Luke, the birth of Jesus and his greatness had been proclaimed to Mary by an angel; and yet it states that his mother and his brothers did not believe in him; then, in contradiction once more, his brother James is called one of his disciples.

No less contradictory are the convictions of the evangelists concerning Jesus' mission and authority: now he is Lord, now servant; now omniscient, now ignorant of the things to come; now he intends the fulfillment of the law of Moses, now he attacks it; now he tramples Satan underfoot, now Satan tempts him and makes him offers. The same uncertainty reigns as to basic doctrines. If in one passage the divinity of Jesus is asserted, in another it is openly denied; if Paul discards works and demands only faith, James states in his Epistle that faith without works is a dead faith. Thus, unresolved contradictions—both as to major points and in narrating individual incidents—misquotations, and misunderstood verses of the Bible abound everywhere. What are we to think of such men as founders of a new faith?

This, in a brief compass, is the content of the second portion of *Ḥizzuḳ Emunah*. Its one hundred chapters are double the number of those in the first part, but it is only a third as long.[60] Despite the decisiveness of rejection, the polemic must be called calm and reasonable in comparison with other works of this genre. The traditional interpretations of every verse of the Bible were familiar to Isaac Troki; his mastery of the material was complete; his biblically-oriented exegesis moderate and sustained by reverence. This justifies the relatively large space devoted (in the sense of a *pars pro toto*) to outlining, while by no means exhausting, the *Ḥizzuḳ Emunah*.

We believe we have outlined the religious convictions of the Jews at the end of the Middle Ages, their controversies and reflections over the problems which had developed over the centuries, following the rise of Christianity and the reversal of their own historical destiny.

V

AN ANTICIPATION
OF THE FUTURE

Isaac Orobio de Castro—
Philipp van Limborch

> Don Balthasar Orobio: De Hippokrates honor,
> de Edom oprovio, de Epicuros horror,
> de la Ley gloria, hace, de sa gran fama eco
> à la historia, Medico Profesor con elegancia,
> y Confesero fiel del Rey de Francia.
>> Daniel Levi de Barrios: Academia de los
>> Floridos, 1685

IN A collection published by Brugsmans-Frank, *Geschiedenis der Joden in Nederland* (Amsterdam, 1940, p. 684), L. Polak has called attention to the only real religious dialogue of the seventeenth century, a dialogue conducted in complete freedom. It took place in Holland in the year 1686. The following year, clothed in the form of a literary correspondence, it appeared as a book bearing the title *De veritate religionis christianae; amica collatio cum eruditio Judaeo* (Gouda, 1687).* The *eruditus Judaeus* was Isaac Orobio de Castro; the Christian, who allowed the book to appear under his name, was Philipp van Limborch.

Philipp van Limborch (1633-1712), professor at the Seminary of the Remonstrants in Amsterdam, had already earned a reputation which endures to the present day as a theologian among the Arminians, that movement within Dutch Calvinism which interpreted more liberally the doctrine of predes-

---

* The Dutch translation of this work which appeared in Amsterdam in 1723 was not available to me.

tination.[61] His opposite number in the dialogue, Isaac Orobio de Castro, is one of the most obscure and, at the same time, most interesting figures of the seventeenth century.[62] Our own interest is limited to the heretofore unexamined doctrinal content of the religious dialogue which the two conducted. Of course, our attention is especially directed to the method of argument used by the Jewish participant, who lacks the support of any tradition of dialogue. We shall be able to reach a better evaluation of his position if we first sketch, however briefly, Isaac Orobio's biography.

Orobio de Castro belonged to the unhappy generation of the Marranos—Jews coerced into baptism in the fifteenth and sixteenth centuries. Jews without roots, Catholics without faith, they sought and found reunion with Judaism. In this process, some men, such as Uriel da Costa, fell victim to a tragic division of conviction, and were shattered; others, such as the physician Juan Prado or the better-known Baruch d'Espinoza, went beyond Judaism to a new world view, pantheistic or, beneath a sublime disguise, atheistic. But the great majority finally succeeded in finding once again a firm footing in Judaism. The community of Spanish Jews in Amsterdam at the middle of the seventeenth century distinguished itself by producing a number of quite important scholars and rabbis of the humanistic school, learned in the secular sciences. I shall mention here Rembrandt's friend Vossius, together with Menasseh ben Israel;[63] the cabalistically oriented Abraham Herera; Juda Leon Templo (the physician in ordinary to the King of Denmark); Benjamin Mussafia; Ḥakam David Cohen de Lara, and many others. Orobio de Castro also belongs to this group, but the course of his life was more troubled than that of all the rest.

Balthasar Orobio de Castro was born in Braganza in 1620. His parents still observed the Day of Atonement in complete secrecy, but otherwise had retained scarcely any mark of Judaism. In Alcala de Henares he studied scholastic philosophy, becoming at Salamanca a secondary-school instructor in metaphysics while pursuing his studies in medicine. He finally became one of the most sought-after physicians in Seville, and physician in ordinary to the Duke of Medina-Celi. He lived in luxury, married, and became a happy paterfamilias. Fate overtook him when the Inquisition turned its attention to him. In work other than their literary dialogue, Philipp van Limborch,[64] basing himself on Orobio's own testimony, narrates his story, which we summarize here:

A Moorish slave whom Orobio had punished for stealing had reported him to the Inquisition as a crypto-Jew. During three years of interrogation he was kept in a narrow, gloomy dungeon belonging to the Inquisition. With gruesome tortures they tried in vain to wring a confession from him. Since he was only suspected, not convicted, of Judaism, he escaped the stake and was condemned to wear publicly for two years the penitent's robe of linen stained with yellow (*sambenito*). Finally he was exiled for the remainder of his life. He went to France, where Louis XIV gave him a professorship of medicine at Toulouse (where many Marranos lived) and the title of Royal Counsellor. About eight years later (1666?), he had come far enough along the path of return that he could confess that he had committed idolatry (*sc.* by embracing Catholicism) and had often been obliged to bow his knee before Baal. With his public avowal of Judaism, he surrendered the Christian name Balthasar for the Jewish Isaac. He went to Amsterdam—Eleutheropolis, city of freedom, it was called then—where, by 1669, he appears on the list of *parnassím* (leaders of the Jewish community). In Amsterdam, in 1685, he founded an Academia de los Floridos for Spanish literature and science. In 1675, when the Portuguese Synagogue was reopened, Rabbi David Zarfati Pina dedicated the opening address to him. As is often the case with converts, he gladly appeared as defender of the doctrines of Judaism; he took this role against the atheistic physician Juan Prado[65] and against Spinoza, whose doctrine he attacked sharply.[66] Finally, also against the Calvinist Philipp van Limborch—a year after their *amica collatio,* originally not meant for the public, he died. As Le Clerc has shown, the publication of their dialogue appeared just before his death, which occurred on November 7, 1687 (1 Kislev 5448).

The title of the work, *De veritate religionis christianae; amica collatio cum erudito Judaeo,*[*] is constructed after the model of Hugo Grotius' famous work. After a "Preface to the Reader," it contains three letters by Orobio—2, 11, and 99 pages long—and three replies by Limborch—3, 31, and 197 pages long. There is an appendix consisting of the famous *Exemplar Vitae Humanae* by Uriel da Costa, with a comment by Limborch. The second portion has nothing to do with the first. The layout of the book must be called unfortunate: there is no trace of a systematically ordered presentation. The unequal lengths of the three pieces is also annoying. The proportion allotted to each of the two disputants is better than two to one in favor of Limborch. But we shall proceed to a description of the content.

The "Preface to the Reader" shows that Limborch is well aware what it means to debate with a Jew, that is, the repre-

---

[*] Orobio's doctrinal debates with Christianity, which interest us here, should actually include also his *Prevenciones Divinas contra la Vana Ydolatria de las Gentes* and his special exegesis of Isaiah 53 and the seventy prophetic weeks of Daniel; but these works exist only in manuscript and are not available to me.[67] There is a work, translated from Spanish into French, called *Israel vengée ou exposition naturelle de prophetes que les chrétiens appliquent à Jesus leur pretendu Messie* (ed. Henriquez, 1770; English edition, Grace Aguilar, London, 1835); but this is hardly original. According to de Rossi (*Bibl. judaica anti-christiana,* Parma, 1800, pp. 86 f.), it made use only of Orobio's ideas. Thus we shall continue to rely on the published exchange of views between him and his friendly enemy Philipp van Limborch.

sentative of a positive faith based on revelation.[68] He praises Orobio's intellect and scholarship beyond measure. He indicates that it is Orobio's intention to show that there are no reasons for a Jew to change his religion, but many arguments to the contrary. Limborch, for his part, will admit to belief in the divine origin of Moses' mission and miracles, but demands of Orobio the same belief in the New Testament accounts of Jesus. Further, he intends to refute his Jewish opponent exclusively with biblical arguments, to draw solely upon the teachings of Christ and the Apostles themselves, disregarding ecclesiastical dogmas.

The first two letters exchanged merely explore the area of dispute. Orobio formulates at the outset the four questions about which the debate is to turn primarily:

1. Where is it written that belief in the Messiah is necessary to salvation for all mankind, so that whoever does not believe in him is damned?

2. Where is it written that the only means of salvation and recovery of God's grace for Israel is faith in a Messiah who has already appeared?

3. Where is it written that Israel has been rejected from its status and honor as people of God, and been dispersed among the nations as punishment for having failed to believe in the Messiah who has appeared?

4. Where is it written that all the prescriptions of the law —except the ethical ones—are to be understood merely as types and prophecies of the future coming of the Messiah?

We can see that these four questions take skillful issue with the central arguments put forward for fifteen hundred years by the literature of the Church *adversus Judaeos.* In fact, every Judaeo-Christian dialogue must deal with these questions. In Orobio's case, their significance lies in the fact that, as a Jew absolutely bound by the Bible, he demands scriptural proof from the Old Testament for the Christian claims. This demand drives his Christian partner into a corner. Limborch is forced to admit that these claims have no literal scriptural support, but are based only upon isolated passages, mostly from the prophets, which can be interpreted in this sense when seen from the viewpoint of the New Testament.

These four questions challenge the Christian to take another look at the solutions offered by Paul and the Apostolic Fathers. Their focus is the messianic problem, defined by Orobio as follows at the end of his second letter: Belief in a messianic redeemer came about through Adam's fall. But only the Jews have knowledge of this; and, in accord with the literal sense of Scripture, their expectation is corporeal; it is an expectation which awaits concrete fulfillment of the prophecies. Jesus could not have been the messianic Saviour, for the simple reason that this "Messiah" had not freed Israel from its enemies, nor restored the ten tribes to their homeland. The Christian belief in the Messiah was something completely different from the Jewish belief. It had no roots in the Torah; it was, instead, the New Revelation contained in the New Testament.

In his long third letter, Orobio discusses in detail the four questions which he had originally raised; but the arguments jump about continually from one question to another, so that a systematic abstract is simply impossible. Since all these questions inevitably issue in the problem of the Messiah, we shall concern ourselves primarily with examining this problem. In I, 6, he develops the theme that, in the Old Testament, God demanded of the Jews faith only in him, not in the Messiah. It was only the New Testament which introduced novel doctrines of the Messiah, differing from the expectation of the Jews. Among contemporary Christians (he continues), only the Chiliasts and Quintomonarchists— *necque pauci, necque indocti, necque Christo infidelis*—retain the proper Old Testament conception: together with the

Jews, they refuse to believe that the prophetic message fore-
telling the future earthly kingdom of Israel or its re-creation
has been already fulfilled by Christ (I, 6).[69] The word of God
has become no clearer through the Gospel than it was before.
It is difficult to dispute against the Christians because they are
divided into so many sects, for what one sect holds to be
orthodox is proscribed by the rest (III, 4). The internal dis-
unity of the many Christian churches and sects over the main
points of the new dispensation proves that Christ has not
made plain what was hidden behind the letter, but rather the
reverse (I, 7). Christ has not given the spiritual meaning of
the letter; but he, at least, unlike the later Church Fathers,
did not shroud the law in mystery. Similarly, the Apostles
generally held to the literal law, as is shown by the example
of Paul (who had Timothy circumcised) or the decision of
the Apostolic Council against the antinomianism of the
Gentile Christians (I, 9).

Even if one proceeds on the basis that the law is to be understood typologically, it could not possibly have been God's
will that the knowledge of the law possessed by the Jews before the coming of the Messiah was only a deception. One
may not read into the Old Testament the concepts and ideas
of a later era, such as Christological doctrines, as though they
had been there from the beginning *in statu nascendi*. All such
ex post facto interpretation is out of order, tendentious, and
does violence to the original meaning of the biblical texts
(I, 11).

It is precisely such a tendentious interpretation to state that
the Jews were punished by God with exile and ruin in spite
of their fidelity to the law, and on account of their firm trust
in the fulfillment of the expectations of their prophets. Christ
certainly did not reject Israel out of hatred or malice. Even on
the Christian hypothesis, the worst that can be assumed is

ignoratia, as even Paul admits, and as Christ expresses with his "Father, forgive them." (I, 12) But Christians must not oversimplify the circumstances, distorting the Jewish messianic expectation in favor of their own system: the Jews await the Messiah not *propter carnalem affectum*—his coming is not necessary for the salvation of the individual's soul! —*sed omnino propter Dei gloriam.* Salvation is already bound up with the law; the work of the Messiah is solely to transform the condition of this world, with its subjection and oppression of the Jews. Together with this external transformation of the world, there will, of course, also be a corresponding inner transformation, the renewal of the heart (I, 17).

In his especially important 17th chapter, Orobio delivers a verdict which must be considered from the point of view of Jewish messianic thought: As far as he can see, the Christian Messiah has not changed men so that they can now love their neighbors more than they could previously. Neither in the conduct of their lives (he continues), nor in the disposition of their hearts, nor in the practice of their religion do I see Christians enjoying a higher spirituality than other peoples, albeit such is a constant source of pride to them (*ibid.,* p. 67). In this man, who had suffered much injustice at the hands of Christians, we can see an anticipation of Voltaire's verdict, and one of Nietzsche's dominant themes: "The Christians must appear more redeemed if I am to believe in their redemption." But Orobio had a greater subjective right to his verdict than did Nietzsche or even Voltaire.

Orobio continues: In place of redemption, we see war, superstition, idolatry, and sectarianism ruling the earth more than ever before. But the blame for all this cannot be placed at the feet of Christianity; indeed, it is counter to the spirit of Christianity. The ethics (*nova lex*), however, which Christianity would like to add to the Jewish law proves incapable of human realization; no Christian lives by the Sermon on the Mount. "If I saw that all Christians had become Capuchin monks, I should be happy to acknowledge this evangelical perfection in contempt of the whole world and everything earthly." (*Ibid.*, p. 67) In any event, the actual condition of Christians justifies nothing more than the Jewish expectation of a future Messiah, since the Jews cannot see that the holy spirit had already been poured out upon mankind. Religious Judaism of the twentieth century could not put the matter any differently.

After making these basic points, Orobio (in I, 18) discusses the Christological interpretation of the prophets. The Old Testament prophets (he says) foretold neither the place nor the time of the Messiah's birth, nor his parents, but only his Davidic descent. And it is just this point about which the Gospels are inconsistent (citing Calvin's remarks about the difficulties raised by Joseph's genealogy). At most, Jesus of Nazareth can be only the Messiah ben Joseph awaited by the Talmud, not the Messiah depicted in the Bible (I, 18).[70]

Even more important, nothing foretold by the prophets concerning the Messiah has been really fulfilled. No sign of the coming of the Kingdom has hitherto been seen, neither among the Gentiles, nor among the Jews, nor in the Christian Church. Even today, God is not known to the majority of the earth's inhabitants. The nations persist in idolatry. Israel is in the same, nay greater, dispersion in which it was before the time of Jesus. Christianity is fragmented into a multitude of sects, and is sunk in idolatry. Depravity rules mankind no less *post* than *ante Christum natum*. The Church of the Popes claims to be the Kingdom of Heaven upon earth, but Israel cannot recognize this. The Roman Church thinks little better of the Reformers than of the Jews, who, for their part, do not feel called upon to settle internal Christian dissension. But Israel itself feels that it stands under a special providence; it recognizes that it is governed by the invisible God. In the miraculous preservation of Israel to the present day, a famous fellow Christian of Limborch has admitted a divine testimony to the close association between Israel and God.[71] Further, he is in agreement with the Christian Chiliasts concerning the future expectation of the Messiah; on this, he cites an interpretation by Cocceius of Ezekiel 37.

In the *secundum et tertium quaesitum* of Orobio we find further extended treatments of the *futura redemptio* of Israel, which we cannot summarize in detail here. He then goes on to show that the Christians misinterpret the prophets. He refers the Servant of God in Isaiah 53 to the entire people of Israel in captivity, in which it must undergo much suffering.[72] But basically he asserts that, for the Jewish faith, the Torah takes precedence over the prophets. It is in the law that God has warned the Israelites not to desert the law, for the law is the proclamation of God's will for his covenanted people. Because of this law, Israel must not believe in an incarnation of God, whom the Torah declares to be invisible to human eyes. Christianity, which erects its faith on the basis of an incarnation which has actually taken place, must be viewed as a form of idolatry.[73] According to Jewish belief, the sin of Adam is atoned for otherwise than through the incarnation of a god-man. The Jewish assurance of redemption, about which Limborch has inquired, rests upon the revelatory miracles contained in the Torah and in the miraculous preservation of Israel down to the present day.

In particular, Orobio affirms the following: The coming of the Messiah was not promised to Israel by God in the sense that he would bring a completely new revelation or proclaim new laws, but rather as a king who would free Israel from oppression of the nations in the Exile (II, 1). Christ was not such a messianic king; this makes untenable the position that Israel has been deprived of certain benefits because of the death of Christ (II, 4). Instead, the suffering with which Israel is punished is explained by its failure to observe the law and its disobedience toward God (II, 7). Neither the Messiah nor a prophet would ever have been able to say anything against the divine law (III, 1). Further, the Messiah is not expected to create a new cultus, since the old "external" one—instituted by God—is already perfect (III, 10).

Replying to the fourth question, Orobio writes that there is indeed a *sensus mysticus* in addition to the *sensus literalis* (IV, 1). The former, though, does not abolish the literal sense of the words, nor have scholars ever elevated it to the status of dogma (IV, 2). The miracles of Moses are without equal (IV, 3), Jewish tradition is infallible (IV, 5), *pace* the Christian denial, the oral law originates from God (IV, 6). Therefore, the course of tradition of the Torah has a higher degree of certainty than that of the Gospel (IV, 8). The laws of the Torah are not to be read allegorically or typologically, least of all as prefigurations. Through them, God made known his will to the generation of the desert, and through this generation, to all generations of Jews. God's will expressed in law is concrete fact, and must be obeyed concretely (IV, 9 ff.).

We have given a fairly comprehensive synopsis of Orobio's position because it is the first time since the dialogue of Justin with the Jew Trypho, more than fifteen hundred years before, that a Jew was allowed to state his views in a Judaeo-Christian debate in full freedom, without censorship by the Church. Great interest attaches to discovering what the Jew has to say to the Christians. Limborch's answers need not here be reproduced *in extenso*[74] because they are not real answers, but, rather, variations on Christian doctrine in the form of a monologue: the sole function of his opponent is to provide the key words. We may summarize, as follows, his point of view regarding the four introductory questions, to which Orobio had given the Jewish answers in his three letters:

To the first question: Contrary to Orobio's denials, faith in Jesus Christ is necessary to salvation for each individual Jew. The Saviour toward whom the prophetic promises of the Old Covenant were directed is descended, on the one hand, from the line of David; on the other, he is a heavenly king with a kingdom "not of this world." Both are fulfilled in Jesus Christ, and only in him.

To the second: The proper understanding of such prophecies as Isaiah 53, Daniel 9:24-27, and other passages of the Old Testament, points to Jesus as the realized Messiah and to his passion.

To the third: Only Israel's murder of Jesus can be the real cause of its punishment through the present misery and endurance of the Exile.

To the fourth: The meaning of Moses' ordinances points beyond the present, as the Old Testament itself declares. The literal interpretation of the laws as service rendered to God through outward ceremonies is repugnant to God. The laws are to be understood typologically and mystically; moreover, the prophets foretold that a new form of worship (*sc.* that of Christ) would replace the Mosaic cultus.

Limborch had preceded these replies to Orobio's four questions with a parallel representation of Moses and Christ (pp. 144-189), designed to show that: (1) Christ's miracles surpass those of Moses, and are more reliably witnessed; (2) the historical evidences for the truth of Christianity are stronger than the traditional evidences for the truth of Judaism; (3) the documents of the New Testament are less corrupt and exhibit a higher degree of inspiration than those of the Old Testament. But it would suffice, he continues, for Orobio to admit only one thing: that in the New Testament a divine revelation is to be found; for, of such a revelation, its conformance in all important points with the Old Testament could easily be proved. Without exception, Limborch's statements describe in outline the process of salvation according to the Christian belief that the prophecies of the Old Testament have been fulfilled in Jesus. In his dispute with Orobio, he renounces any claim to originality and allies himself completely with the traditional method of scriptural proof used by the ancient Church.[75] The propriety of this position he had discussed previously in his major doctrinal work, *Institutiones Theologiae Christianae* (Amsterdam, 1686, I, III, 27), in which he displays affinities to Cocceius' mode of thought, particularly in his belief in the gradual process of revelation.

In spite of the brevity of our summary, Limborch's own theology should at least be delineated with adequate clarity. It is erected upon the essential conviction that Jesus was greater than Moses because he was not only a prophet like him, but also Messiah. This was all, according to Limborch, that was meant by the title, "Son of God." He was not himself God, as the Jews suspected the Christians of claiming. Characteristically, on this point he appeals to Erasmus and the luminaries of his own Arminian religious party, Episcopius and Hugo Grotius (*ibid.,* pp. 198, 218, 243).

This strong emphasis on Jesus' messianic office must be seen as a specifically Arminian characteristic. In the same manner, we must understand Limborch's restricting conviction that Christians need believe only what is written in the New Testament, particularly in the Gospels, in order to be saved. This separation of New Testament Christianity from subsequent periods of doctrinal development is also found in the English philosopher John Locke, who was a close personal friend of Limborch. In theology, Locke represented a rationalistic supernaturalism.[76] Insofar as Locke advocated the ideas of tolerance, motivated by Christian principles which were current at the time of Cromwell's revolution, he could look only with favor upon any Judaeo-Christian *amica collatio.*[77] Indeed, Locke's *A Letter Concerning Toleration* is dedicated to Philipp van Limborch!

To this sketch of the positions of both participants in the conversation we should add, finally, a few individual observations and more general remarks. The first thing to attract attention is the fact that Orobio, a Jew, almost never refers to Talmudic and rabbinic evidence. His unfamiliarity with Hebrew may account for this. His style of argument is purely biblical, and is supported only now and then by examples drawn from the history of Spain and the Spanish Jews.[78] He exhibits an often amazing familiarity with the history of Christianity, especially its heresies. For his part, Philipp van Limborch has, through his study of the history of the Inquisition, a remarkably complete knowledge of the history of the Jews in Spain. He speaks accurately of the situation of the Marranos, when he affirms that the Spanish Jews teach their children that it suffices to be a Jew at heart, even without explicit avowal, and that God's written law is not transgressed if one is a Jew only in one's soul, even though outwardly conforming to the requirements of Roman Catholicism (*ibid.,* pp. 275 f.). He is well informed also about the contemporary Sephardic Judaism of Holland, several times quoting its most celebrated spokesman, Manasseh ben Israel (*ibid.,* pp. 154, 221; and *passim*). He also mentions the appearance of Sabbatai Zevi, whom he calls *Messiam ridiculum* (*ibid.,* p. 163). He likewise has access to the classic

Bible commentaries of the rabbis and refers repeatedly to Ibn Ezra, Maimonides, and Rashi. Nevertheless, he, too, endeavors (according to the preface in which he sets forth his program) to conduct an argument based strictly on the Bible.

In spite of his long-winded discussion of many details, Limborch never succeeded in engaging in real *dialogue* with Orobio. The time was not yet ripe for genuine conversation between the faiths. In this *amica collatio,* two religious realities were set beside each other in the form of monologues. True religious dialogue is a development of the twentieth century. Even in Holland—the classical land of religious freedom, and on the doorstep of the age of toleration—only one *amica collatio* was possible, a unique event without consequence.

After his own fashion, Isaac Orobio de Castro was a good representative of the Jewish religious system, especially when one reckons to his credit the fact that he could not speak on behalf of the full reality of Judaism, but only from the abbreviated reality of an apostate's re-espousal of his ancestral faith. Especially in his criticism of the New Testament and its miracles, which we have overlooked in this study as being of less importance, his views are in remarkable agreement with those advanced against Christianity by the Polish Karaite Isaac Troki. It is hardly possible, however, that Orobio knew of the *Ḥizzuḳ Emunah.*

In my view, the most important service Orobio rendered, which assures him his place in this history of Judaeo-Christian religious dialogue, was to be an early representative of modern man, to undertake the first modest attempts at examining the positions from which Judaism and Christianity confronted each other. The essence of his apologetic and polemic statements resides—it seems to me—in the fact that he saw one thing clearly and spoke it plainly: even though Jews and Christians have the same concepts and terms, such as revelation, redemption, Messiah, restoration, and so on, for the most part they use these with different content, because the postulates of the Jewish faith differ from those of Christianity. Those of Judaism rest upon the covenant and the election of a single nation, both of which continue in force despite all the blasts of secular history. Those of Christianity rest upon the redemptive act of a single man, who, according to Christian doctrine, was also God. Philipp van Limborch did not understand this difference; nor, in that era, could he have. Nevertheless, he must be credited with having striven for an objectivity and dispassionateness which are not too common in this sort of debate.

On this occasion, Limborch allowed the specifically Arminian doctrines which he developed in his theological works to take a back seat to those common to Christianity in general.[79] He did this in order to put belief in Christ as the redeemer sent by God upon a biblical foundation, and to give the universal Christian answers to the polemic questions of the Jew. Yet he has been accused of not restraining sufficiently his Arminian principles, and hidden attacks upon orthodoxy have been charged to his account.[80] But it was precisely the fact that Limborch was an Arminian, that he was much more open to the postulates of religious toleration than were the orthodox, which allowed him to participate at all in this debate.[81]

Finally, one's verdict on Orobio would be that his realistic expectation of the Messiah and his protest against Christian exegesis of the Old Testament are a legitimate representation of Judaism. He protested against what Friedrich Nietzsche has called "a monstrous farce: to pull the Old Testament out from under the Jews with the contention that it contains nothing but Christian doctrine."[82] Orobio's "corporeal" interpretations of Old Testament prophecies did not gain the enthusiastic applause of Christian Chiliasts by accident.[83] Meyer Kayserling's evaluation of him[84] is certainly valid: "None of his contemporaries attacked the basic doctrines of Christianity with more vigor than he." Opinions will differ whether the following judgment is also justified: "Few refuted these doctrines with such erudition and precision."

VI

TURNING POINT: THE MODERN ERA

1 MOSES MENDELSSOHN

IF THE debate between the Jewish and Christian faiths is pursued through the centuries, the decisive caesura in its history must probably be placed at the close of the eighteenth century. At this time the first Jews were seized by the spirit of modernism; and, with the opening of the ghetto gates, a last remnant of the Middle Ages vanished from modern Europe. It is well known that within a few decades—the life span of one generation—the Jews caught up with the developments of three centuries: the length of time it took the Christian West to pass from a theonomously determined sacral culture to the emancipation of man and belief in him as a creative center of reality. In the figure of Moses Mendelssohn (1729-1786)—apart from the exceptional case of Baruch Spinoza—the first intellectually emancipated Jew came on the scene late in the Age of Enlightenment. No sooner had "that philosophical Jew Moses Mendelssohn" (as he was called in an obscure rejoinder by a Jesuit, Benedict Stattler) come into view than he was immediately called to account by an enraged Christian. The inner motivation of the controversy between Moses Mendelssohn and Johann Caspar Lavater is today fairly clear.[85] As something entirely new in the history of these debates, it is of exemplary importance: for the first time, one can speak of "toleration," of "understanding," and of "mutual appreciation."

At this point in history, a change took place from the thought of the Middle Ages to that of the Enlightenment, from belief in suprarational revelation to belief in reason treated as a metaphysical entity. The importance of this change for philosophical and theological thought has been described in detail in another place;[86] it had an important consequence for this history of religious dialogue. For the first time, men took seriously the problem of the multiplicity of existing religions and the question of the share each had in what must itself be unique, the universal truth. To the Middle Ages, it would have seemed an absurd and unthinkable idea that another extant religion, *concurrently* with one's own, could represent a portion of the truth; only the modern relativizing tendency allowed this thought even to arise. We must not be deceived into believing that the situation had been otherwise by the relative degree of recognition granted to Christianity by the religious law, or by occasional speculations of Judah ha-Levi, Maimonides, and others about the historical purpose of Christianity (cf. *Geschichte der jüd. Religionsphilosophie*, p. 77). In the last analysis, Christians and Moslems were viewed as people who had strayed from the truth.[87]

All the debates discussed in the previous chapters were ultimately hostile in nature. They had the apologetic, or polemic, purpose of substantiating the truth of one's own doctrines and justifying those believing in them. They were far from taking in the least seriously any claim to truth which the belief of someone else might have. Neither *Kuzari* nor any of the medieval "disputations" led to genuine *dialogue.* Admittedly, neither did the controversy between Lavater and Mendelssohn, but it represents a transitional stage on the road to genuine dialogue, such as has become possible in the twentieth century. In this sense, we can already speak here of "progress," the more so since the theological controversies we have described, although running their course at a high level, were carried on in previous periods much more primitively a few levels lower. For the most part, Jews were looked upon as "religious criminals," as "evil and hardhearted men," who crucified "our Lord and Saviour Jesus Christ." When the authorities let the fanatical mobs loose in the streets, this deed was revenged hundreds of times over on the persons and goods of the Jews. In the course of centuries, more than a single ghetto went up in flames, and not once only. The Jews could not revenge themselves in deed against their powerful tormentors, but took vengeance in word and writing. The apocryphal *Toledot Jeshu* ("Generations of Jesus"), with its bitter and stinging mockery of Christianity and its founder (which went through many editions and was widely circulated among the lower classes, frequently being read on Christmas Eve), is an important source for ascertaining the temper of the oppressed Jewish masses of those centuries. We must not lose sight of this background, nor of the true "significance" of the religious debates between clergy and rabbis at the courts of medieval rulers. As their outcome, the king or prince in question usually promised himself an occasion for a pogrom, for the purpose of justifiable (!) expropriation of Jewish wealth. This must be kept in mind if we are to evaluate properly the significance of the Enlightenment for the Jews, the ideological value of toleration, and the enormous achievement of emancipations, as well as the first encounter with the ancient foe in the clear air of freedom—

that is, the Lavater-Mendelssohn controversy. If we keep the background in mind, the scanty contribution of this first modern dialogue to the solution of the problem can be excused. It is no surprise that all the arguments pro and con, already traditional, brought forward in this debate, seem worn and hackneyed. In spite of this, one can understand what a feeling of exaltation must have filled the Jewish participant upon this occasion, the first time the disputants crossed swords upon an equal footing, with all of educated Europe as bystanders.

In French Switzerland, Charles Bonnet, a representative of the local "rational orthodoxy," had published a work called *Palingenesie Philosophique*. Its apologetic portions had been translated into German by Johann Caspar Lavater under the title *Herrn Charles Bonnets Untersuchung der Beweise für das Christentum etc.* On the basis of earlier conversations, Lavater added to the German edition a "communication" addressed to Moses Mendelssohn. It was dated August 25, 1769, and publicly challenged Mendelssohn either to refute these proofs of Christianity or, if he could not, to draw the proper conclusions. This public challenge brought great distress to Mendelssohn, who was still by no means comfortably at home in the educated world of Europe. It came from the pen of the same Lavater who could declare a bit later in his *Physiognomischen Fragmenten*: "It is senseless to force *one* form of religion upon the conscience of a nation, congregation, or society. Coercion can force a man to outward agreement, but not to inner conviction." (III, 240)

It is not our task to trace the course of this dispute, in which posterity has judged Mendelssohn to have played a more worthy role than Lavater, whose motives were ambiguous. Our purpose is to evaluate the outcome of the debate. Nevertheless, we must recognize one of the motives behind

Lavater's challenge, for he was a fanatical enthusiast for Christianity, whose eagerness to make converts did not stop short of Goethe, Rousseau, and others. His attention to Mendelssohn was aroused by the fact that, in spite of every inclination toward the cosmopolitan, universal religion of reason characteristic of the age, a Jew who had achieved a respected position in Christian intellectual life continued to hold tenaciously to a *particularistic* form of religion. The "Jewish philosopher in Berlin" would not be converted; however, since he could no longer remain silent, he engaged in an exchange of correspondence with Bonnet and Lavater. The publication of these letters, as they were exchanged over a period of two years, attracted the excited attention of Europe, brought about the intervention of Friedrich Nicolai, "the squabbler-prince of the Holy Roman Empire," and, when it was over, provoked Johann Georg Hamann, Georg Christoph Lichtenberg, Matthias Claudius, Pastor Kölbele, and many others to express their views. Mendelssohn's side of this debate was further clarified by the publication, thirteen years later, of the work *Jerusalem oder über religiöse Macht und Judentum* (Jerusalem or Concerning Religious Power and Judaism) (1783). His position was made doubly difficult by the fact that he did not want to violate the principle of toleration in religious matters, a principle which he had himself championed. This point of view was somewhat later clothed in literary form by his friend Lessing in the play *Nathan the Wise*. Further, political caution bade him refrain from religious controversies of whatever sort, for he knew that he was "a member of an oppressed people, which must beg protection from the good will of the ruling nation, not everywhere receiving it, nor receiving it anywhere without certain limitations." (VII, 14) He reminds Lavater that Jews are not even granted residence in Zürich. How could the Jews of Prussia dare declare war on the religion of their protectors, that is, "attack them from the side which must be most sensitive in virtuous men"?

But the heart of the difficulty lies deeper; to discuss it leads directly to the essence of the matter. It turns out that Moses Mendelssohn, as humanist and man of the Enlightenment, can no longer by faith hold certain positions represented by all rabbis and scholars before him. Thus in the course of the public debate, he was forced by Lavater to give his views on the person of Jesus and his condemnation by the Jewish Sanhedrin. On this point (in the last private letter to Lavater, dated January 15, 1771), he gives the following attenuated answer, to which the disputants of the Middle Ages could hardly have given assent: "It seems as though we are forever being called to account for this [*sc.* the wrong committed by the Sadducees and Pharisees against the person of Jesus]. How should I know what just or unjust verdicts were delivered by my ancestors 1,700 to 1,800 years ago in Jerusalem?" (VII, 362) He cannot even assume responsibility for the Royal Prussian Courts of his own day. In any case, lacking first-hand accounts, he refuses to give an opinion in this matter. Further, he has the pleasure of knowing many fellow Jews who possess this wise moderation, not taking upon themselves the liberty of committing blasphemy. Now a completely new tone is heard: "I also know quite a few who, together with me, go even further: on the evidence of Christian witnesses they are prepared to acknowledge the innocence of the founder of that religion, as well as the moral goodness of his character." (*Ibid.*) Along with this, of course, he makes the *traditional* conditions: Jesus never intended to set himself on the same level as the Father, never tried to pass himself off as a divine person, never laid claim for himself to the honor of worship, and never intended to overthrow the

religion of his fathers. It is interesting to note that these conditions are not put forth in the traditional spirit, insisting that
the truth of God and of the revelation to Israel depended
upon them. They are put forth in the spirit of the Enlightenment, which elevates the moral excellence of intentions to the
status of an ultimate standard of judgment. He writes further: "The conditions are absolutely necessary. In fact, if
several suspect discourses and utterances had to be taken in
the literal sense, the judgment on the moral excellence of his
intentions would take a completely different turn." (*Ibid.*)

It is not surprising, given the moderating effect of the
philosophy of the Enlightenment upon various central concepts of Jewish theology, that Mendelssohn's fervent desire
for toleration and his striving for harmonization were not
pursued by simply ignoring basic *Christian* doctrines.* Indeed, in this regard, Mendelssohn merely shares with other
Christian philosophers of the Enlightenment the views of his
age. For example, he disposes of the doctrine of the vicarious
atonement of Jesus upon the premises of his rational philosophy with the remark, "In God's economy no individual suffers merely for the good of others." (VII, 73) The *Gegenbetrachtungen* (1770), provoked by the dispute with Lavater
and aimed directly at Bonnet; numerous letters of these
years; and the relevant portions of the late work *Jerusalem*—
all these show clearly that Mendelssohn saw Judaism's advantage over the Christian religion precisely in its lack of any
positively obligatory doctrine based on faith, transcending
reason.[88] In a very revealing letter written to the hereditary
Prince of Brunswick at the beginning of 1700, Mendelssohn
expressly transfers the "shibboleth" of religion from the "historical truth of the mission" to the "logical truth of the doc-

* See our *Geschichte der jüdischen Religionsphilosophie in der Neuzeit* ("History of
Jewish Religious Thought in Modern Times") for a discussion of the impact of
the Enlightenment upon the thought of Mendelssohn.

trine." On this basis he discards the Trinity, the Incarnation, Christ's life of suffering and atoning death; "they appear diametrically opposed to the basic postulates of human knowledge." (VII, 301) The basic difference, then, between the books of the Old and of the New Testament consists in Mendelssohn's contention that "the former are in harmony with my philosophical convictions, or at least are not opposed to them; the latter, on the contrary, demand a faith of which I am incapable." (*Ibid.*)

As we have seen, Ḥasdai Crescas (in *Biṭṭul 'Iḳḳere ha-Noṣrim*) (The Refutation of the Christian Dogmas) and Joseph Albo (in *'Iḳḳarim*) forged their weapons for the refutation of Christianity out of the circumstance that, in its central doctrines, Christianity contradicted the reasonable but severely supernatural Old Testament concept of revelation. Three hundred years later, because he was ultimately only a Jewish philosopher of the religion of the Enlightenment, the first Jewish systematic theologian of the modern era believed that he had "refuted" Christianity (in his *Gegenbetrachtungen*) through the fact that, in contrast to the Jewish faith, which nowhere "disagrees with reason," the Christian revelation cannot be proved and verified by natural human reason (VII, 91 ff.; cf. also the Alt edition of *Jerusalem,* Ges. Schr. III, 129-133).

Yet another aspect is significant for evaluating the transformation in attitude toward the Christian religion. This is the fact of ethical-religious universalism, which became possible only through the Enlightenment. In the unusually revealing letter to the Prince of Brunswick which immediately precedes the January, 1770, edition of the *Gegenbetrachtungen* directed at Bonnet, the champion of reason and undogmatic toleration, drawn into a religious dispute against his will, agrees to the following, almost programmatic, statement: "Since the creator intended all men for eternal bliss, an exclusive religion cannot be the true one. I venture to state this as a criterion for truth in religious matters. No revelation purporting to be alone capable of saving man can be the true revelation, for it does not harmonize with the purposes of the all-merciful creator." (VII, 302) Thus Mendelssohn expressed unambiguously his views on a problem which could seem a *problem* only to a Jew of the Enlightenment: what is to become of the millions upon millions of inhabitants of the earth if only a single group of people is deemed worthy of salvation and blessedness? The Talmudists and rabbis of the Middle Ages had had a ready answer to this question. The god-fearers among the Gentiles, who kept the Noachite laws, would partake of the future world, together with the Israelites. They scarcely bothered to reflect further upon the matter. For the purposes of religious law, they classified Christianity and Islam under the category of *shittûph* (dependent and derivative religion). They had so little doubt of the *unique* nature of truth (as opposed to all kinds of syncretism), bound up with the covenant and gracious election of the Jewish nation, that they could not be disturbed by the question of the ultimate salvation of the Gentiles. But Mendelssohn *is* disturbed, especially when confronted with this question mark. And so he declares solemnly that "an exclusive religion cannot be the true one," that a revelation valid for only a part of mankind can only be particularistic; whereas the all-wise goodness of God cannot allow the rest of mankind to remain without revelation. "All inhabitants of the earth are called to blessedness, and the means to this end are [therefore] as widespread as mankind itself." (*Jerusalem,* III, 215) According to Mendelssohn, there is a universal source of knowledge (in this setting, presumably Jewish, actually belonging to the Enlightenment) for the blessedness prepared by God for the human race: *reason*. For him, Judaism is completely identical with reason. Its basic rational principles, which are equally valid for all men, were only supplemented and extended by certain events of history (the revelation upon Sinai) and the particular ritual and ceremonial laws which refer to these events. In themselves, the latter are binding and cannot be abrogated, but only the Jews are obliged to obey and follow them in detail. The postulates of natural religion without revelation, valid for all Gentile mankind, "are legible and comprehensible to all men through the creation and its inner proportion." (III, 315) According to the outline of his philosophical system, these postulates are identical in his eyes with his historical Jewish religion. This special revelation only imposed additional special obligations upon a particular portion of mankind.

Does this mean that a special revelation is basically unnecessary? Mendelssohn actually asks this question and gives an affirmative answer, at least "for all the nations which have had none." It is true that God gave the Israelites a revelation, "not because men as men cannot achieve blessedness without revelation, but because his wise purpose required that this special people be honored with a special grace.... Henceforth this people is no longer allowed to seek its salvation by any other way than that which God has ordained for it."[89] But "all other peoples of the earth can and must live and attain salvation according to the light of nature." And, with all the optimism of the confident Enlightenment: "If the degree of enlightenment of a people admits, all truths necessary to the salvation of the human race ultimately can be constructed upon knowledge gained by reason." (*Gegenbetrachtungen*, VII, 75) Of course, there is an immediate objection that Jewish ritual and ceremonial laws do not correspond with reason.

Mendelssohn replies with the statement that this is only apparently so; in reality, "all laws refer to or are based upon eternal rational truths, or remind us of them and awaken us to reflection upon them." (*Jerusalem*, III, 321)

It does not need to be pointed out to a reader with even the least bit of knowledge that this conception of Judaism, which became epoch-making for Jewish liberalism of the nineteenth century, omitted the very *heart* of Judaism: the *living God*, who, without consideration for reason and "ability to gain agreement" (which *Morgenstunden*, VII defines as the highest form of suitability) has acted in the history of this nation; who, above all, revealed not only laws but also doctrines, such as the doctrine of creation *ex nihilo*. Typically, Mendelssohn reduced this conception to the abstraction of a first efficient cause.[90] Nor can we be surprised that his treatment of the positive points of Christian doctrine is even less satisfactory. In *Gegenbetrachtungen*, in the letter to the Prince, and in other contexts, he strives to demonstrate the irrationality or preterrationality of the Christian doctrines of the Trinity, original sin, the incarnation, redemption through Christ, the resurrection, the ascension, and so forth. These doctrines cannot provide for the human race "necessary conditions for salvation." This polemic is based on the rejection of Christological passages from the Bible, which are intended to incline "a philosopher living under the Mosaic law" to accept the witness of the New Testament.[91] But even this remains mild and conciliatory. Indeed, Mendelssohn even expresses the hope that, according to the "views of several excellent men (*sc.* the English Deists and Unitarians), who have the best intentions toward truth and the Christian religion, all these statements which seemingly are repugnant to sound reason will be explained as human additions." (VII, 301)[92]

This is not exactly what took place. But his students and many of the next generation drew the proper conclusions, albeit unwillingly, from Mendelssohn's emptying the faith of content. This faith was bound to a ceremonial law as a form divested of its content; and this law itself (thirty years later!) the faith was most willing to surrender as the price for political emancipation—and not only the ceremonial law, but also the entire religion of the fathers was to be surrendered without hesitation, to the degree that such could take place "without encroaching upon its reasonableness, without injuring moral sensitivity."[93] This was the last *reservatio mentalis* against conversion which could be made by the disciples of a utilitarian rationalism, uprooted from the Jewish faith and historical consciousness, not least through Mendelssohn's influence. In contrast to his descendants and disciples, Moses Mendelssohn maintained sincerely his devout personal life, and strictly observed the religious law, because to him it still meant the divine guarantee of "salvation." (Cf. the statements in *Jerusalem*, III, 350 f.) He himself remained aware that "our reasonings can never free us from the strict obedience we owe to the law." (*Ibid.*, p. 356)

In regard to the Judaeo-Christian religious dispute fought out in the exchange of correspondence with Lavater and Bonnet, the first of the modern era, our verdict must be that only superficial "contentions" and "refutations" were made. This was a result of the fatal abbreviation undergone by the doctrines of both religions, which has its ultimate explanation in the spirit of the age. Nevertheless, this dispute is a landmark of progress. For the first time, tradition-conscious Judaism, which entered the intellectual arena of modern Europe in the figure of Mendelssohn, was confronted with the full import of the question: How could its claim to absolute religious truth be brought into agreement with the similar claims of the religions which ruled this arena? After this first encounter, and after the disgraceful capitulation of Mendelssohn's pupils, this question became all the more pressing.

2 SALOMON FORMSTECHER

Seventy years later, a Jew once more undertook to come to a basic understanding with the Christian religion, to assign it a place in his philosophical world view. This took place in a world already far removed from Moses Mendelssohn and the Enlightenment. In the meantime, the idea of the emancipation of the Jews had prevailed, and had to a large extent become reality. The second generation to grow up in the context of German intellectual life and in a cultural milieu determined by Christianity was in the prime of life. Furthermore, this German intellectual life and the consciousness of reality characteristic of the period had, under the aegis of Kantian philosophy and the classical systems of German idealism, gone through a far-reaching transformation with respect to the Enlightenment. In addition, the position which Judaism claimed for itself in a society defined by unsecularized Christian thought had changed for the Christian bourgeois class of the mid-nineteenth century.

Kant had still seen Judaism, through the eyes of Spinoza and under the influence of Mendelssohn, as revealed legislation.[94] Schelling and Hegel had utilized the Christian doctrine of the Logos in founding and erecting a universal system of thought. In their eyes, the Logos possessed a speculative meaning which transcended dry rationalism and, at least, paid more respect to its content. Especially in Hegel's *Philos-*

ophy of Religion, Judaism was accorded a place in the history of mankind and religion appropriate to its "idea" (according to Hegel). It preserved this status in the eyes of the Christian bourgeoisie for more than fifty years, perhaps almost to the present day, even though scarcely ten years after Hegel's death there was almost nothing genuine left of the imposing edifice erected by the universalistic philosopher and state thinker of Prussia.

According to Hegel's theory, Judaism was "a religion born in affliction and for the afflicted." In the logical unfolding of the Hegelian Idea, it was an example of "negativity"; it represented a lower stage of religion to be transcended in the course of history. Judaism was the stage of "exaltation," in which the Spirit is present "only as a general concept," remaining unknown in its proseity outside of Israel. To the awareness of the blindly dependent, God appears only as something alien, something external, which, as pure negativity, seems to be *contra naturam* (*vide* the image of an angry God). Christianity, on the other hand, represents the religion of perfect reconciliation between God and man.[95]

Even after the speculative philosophical elements of the system had been laid aside, the spirit of this theory long remained alive. As a result, during the course of the nineteenth century, there arose the idea that Judaism was dead, that it had long been superseded; it was no longer necessary to discuss it seriously. Paradoxically, the only thing left of Judaism was the Jews themselves, who, therefore, should be evangelized and assimilated as soon as possible. In contrast with all previous dogmatic distinctions and refutations, from the Church Fathers through the Schoolmen and Reformers down to Lavater, since the time of Hegel's speculative edifice of the history of religion on the basis of the Idea (Logos), the problem had been considered solved. The impressive systematic endeavors of Salomon Formstecher (1808-1889) and Samuel Hirsch (1815-1889) were unable to alter the situation, especially since they appeared only ten years after the actual end of the formative period of absolute idealism. This historical delay has remained a characteristic of all the endeavors of emancipated Judaism up to this day. As a result, they were no longer able to capture the sustained attention of either the Christian or the Jewish public. Nevertheless, from the standpoint of the historian of religion, they must be considered an estimable contribution to the controversy with speculative idealistic philosophy, and their fertilization of the Jewish area of research must be accounted valuable.[96] S. Hirsch's *Religionsphilosophie der Juden* (Leipzig, 1842) is of lesser importance for the history of Judaeo-Christian religious dialogue; but S. Formstecher's *Religion des Geistes* (Leipzig, 1841) marks a change—the most radical, in fact, which ever occurred, or ever became possible as a consequence of the postulates of speculative thought.[97] Completely reversing historical conditions and totally neglecting doctrinal and historical circumstances, Formstecher declares Judaism to be the true world religion, explaining the role of the Christian Church as that of being the Jewish world mission. We shall sketch briefly how, following in the footsteps of Schelling's philosophy of identity, Formstecher accomplished this feat even, given his assumptions, being able to make it credible.

Formstecher views the course of history as determined by an original polarity—paganism and Judaism—corresponding to the polar duality within which Schelling sees the "world-soul" unfold. Paganism is an "aesthetic manifestation of the absolute," the religion of the deification of nature, possessing solely an "ideal of universal life." Therefore, it came to a halt at the culminating stage of its development, as soon, that is, as it arrived at the degree of self-awareness of which it was capable. It was then resolved into Judaism, the "religion of the spirit," so that the dualism of the religious life might be resolved into a unity within the subject, the vehicle of the spirit (*Religion des Geistes,* p. 363). But since this will happen only at the end of history, when the "relative" truth of Judaism has finally become "absolute" truth, "throughout the course of history, paganism and Judaism must develop alongside each other as hostile opposites, continuing to advance until each religion, in its own sphere, has recognized and realized its ideal." (*Ibid.,* p. 70) Thus Judaism has its own course of development from imperfection to perfection; at every stage it has a mission to paganism, a mission which remains forever constant, but proceeds from different causes at different times. Thus Judaism displays a twofold history: a development within itself and also a development of its relationship to mankind. God's will does not grant it a direct influence upon paganism in the sense of immediate involvement.[98] Instead, Christianity and Islam appear upon the scene as "transitory representatives of that aspiring influence, on their own part simultaneously bearing witness to the truth of the 'religion of the spirit.' Christianity and Islam are the bearers of the mission of Judaism; they mediate the course of mutual interaction between Judaism and mankind [paganism], bringing the latter to self-awareness of the spirit." The nature of the mission is a movement of Judaism out of itself through paganism and then back upon itself, according to the form of the reflexive, cognitive act, which, as a movement of the subject, passes through the object and returns upon itself. (*Ibid.,* p. 365)

Formstecher's actual purpose can now be seen, *why* he transferred to Judaism Schelling's speculative philosophy of identity, oblivious to even the grossest incongruities and contradictions. The reason is this: by extending and applying Schelling's principle of identity to the history of Judaism, he sought to prove that its "religion of the spirit" was, in fact, the religion of absolute truth. "When the spirit has passed through the first stage of its development, when it has accomplished the awareness of its subjective character in Judaism through recognition of the ideal of its individual life, it begins the second part of its endeavor, the struggle for identification. It can present this actively only through Judaism; paganism must show itself purely passive and self-sacrificing. Thus Judaism must emerge from its isolation and show mankind its life. . . . During the second part of its life, during its struggle to identify the subjective and the objective, the spirit must assert and maintain the awareness it has achieved as something subjective. At the same time, it must exert its influence upon the objective, so that the latter may finally merge into unity with the subjective. The spirit presents this twofold goal in the following manner: It causes Judaism to appear as the perpetual representative of its self-awareness, and Judaism's mission to paganism as the transitory representative of that effort to influence the objective. Judaism finds all attempts to win proselytes contradictory to its essential nature, because it is called upon to represent its truth, not to put it into effect. But it is precisely at this point that the mission of Judaism [*sc.* Christianity and Islam] sees its task: it is called upon to introduce the truth of Judaism into mankind and win dominion for it." (*Ibid.,* pp. 363 f.)

The "Jewish" missionary task of Christianity is this: "to elevate the spirit from its life as a universal to a life as an individual, to bring it back to itself after its absorption into nature, to redeem it from this defection from itself, to reconcile it once more with itself. The living symbol of this redemption and reconciliation is seen by Christianity in the death of Jesus, in which mankind was shown how nature must be subordinated and subjected to the spirit, paganism to Judaism." (*Ibid.,* p. 369) Clearly, Formstecher concedes nothing to Schelling, Hegel, and their theological disciples in the Protestant camp in reinterpreting and transforming creeds and historical facts.[99] In his case, however, these reinterpretations follow from his interest in the Jewish historical viewpoint. Especially charming is the tour de force by which he interprets Christianity's claim to absolute truth as a misunderstanding of its "Jewish" mission: "Christianity shows its absolute truth in this effort to develop from its absorption in the life of nature into its true self, from its life as universal to its life as individual; for in this effort it proclaims itself the mission of Judaism. But it shows its relative, purely transitory truth, in the fact that it celebrates the beginning of the resolution of its task as the end, erroneously vindicating itself as an absolute, independent entity." In order to celebrate the absolute truth of the only "religion of the spirit" in the relative truth of its offshoots, Formstecher reinterprets all Christian doctrines as necessary characteristics of this mission. We must admit that he does this very skillfully. According to him, it was gratifying that "as a result of its missionary task, Christianity had to disguise the 'spiritual process' in the garments of paganism . . . so that the latter might recognize it as a demand arising from its own life, and, as such, achieve it. Thus at its inception, Christianity appeared in the pagan costume of pantheism, which deifies the human spirit, thus proclaiming the identity of God with the world. It was no longer the human spirit which was to be redeemed and reconciled; rather, the spirit of God undertook this work of redemption. He himself offered himself in order to satisfy his righteousness, which demanded an atoning sacrifice on account of the fall of man through original sin, and also in order to satisfy his love, which could no longer allow mankind to abide in the misery of sin." (*Ibid.,* p. 373) This extremely detailed reinterpretation of the doctrines of the Christian faith serves to demonstrate its relative missionary task and the absolute nature of Judaism. The crowning verdict is that "Christianity has veiled the ethic of Judaism in the metaphysics of paganism in order to realize organically its missionary task." (*Ibid.,* p. 374)

As a mission, Christianity was sent primarily to the northern world "so that paganism might be transformed into Judaism by the aid of that philosophy of freedom which is native to the northern lands." (*Ibid.,* p. 398) For the south, another means, "conditioned by the locale," was necessary: Islam, which, unlike Christianity, represents not "religious philosophy" but "religious poetry. . . . In the objective process of the unfolding of the spirit, Christianity denotes the element which looses itself from the bonds of nature, demanding absolute freedom. Islam, likewise, points to the element which extricates itself from the realm of nature, but it achieves this transition not by means of freedom, but by means of unthinking submission. Islam is in slavish subjection to the despotic demand of God; whoever represents this subjection in his thoughts and actions is a Moslem." (*Ibid.,* p. 399) This unachievable amalgamation of Jewish freedom with pagan "fate" gives rise to the Jewish-pagan character of the mission to the southern portion of mankind which can only be called "Islamic."

But when Christianity and Islam have fulfilled their mission, that is, when the progress of the spirit toward the goal set before it has reached its end, when all pagan mankind has been proselytized and won to the God of Judaism, then, according to Formstecher, both transitory representatives of the religion of the spirit will have reverted once more to Judaism. Formstecher expresses this process as follows, describing the inner development of Christianity: "When Christianity has recognized that it is to reconcile men not with God, with whom they are already reconciled through his all-goodness, but rather with its own spirit, from which it has become estranged through its worship of nature; when it realizes that Christianity must be viewed only as a mission of Judaism to paganism, but not at all to Judaism itself . . . only then has it organically recast the pagan element within itself into the Jewish, only then has it—qualitatively speaking—accomplished its mission and realized a kingdom of heaven upon earth." (*Ibid.,* pp. 394 f.) In that hour, Christianity will have fulfilled its transitory purpose in the development of mankind. It may be noted that Formstecher and religious liberalism understood the messianic age, not traditionally, having its inception in a catastrophe of history, but rather as a product of upward development. On the eve of this age, Christianity will return once more to Judaism, in order to fulfill the word of the prophet: "And many nations shall join themselves to the Lord in that day, and shall be My people." (Zech. 2:15)

Enabled by the speculative philosophy of history peculiar to the Age of Idealism, Formstecher solved the problem of the historical coexistence of Israel and Christianity by saying that Christianity was called to be that powerful expression of the "world-soul" which was *allowed* to represent the truth in hybrid form, to missionize the world for Judaism. This was done to free Judaism from a direct missionary duty. Between them both hovers the unfortunate concept, borrowed from Johann Fichte, of "mutual interaction." The question of the universal validity of Judaism receives a satisfactory answer; as a result of this system, Judaism can continue in its primal purity.[100] This idea of an indirect missionary role played by Christianity and Islam throughout the whole world was not exactly unthinkable to the Middle Ages. What *was* unthinkable (and therefore characterizes the basic change vis-à-vis the parallel ideas of Judah ha-Levi and Maimonides) was the rational incorporation of all historical events into one systematic principle. This principle, declaring necessary those events and developments which actually partake only of the nature of possibility, has its real meaning only at the end of history. In other words, a philosophical representative of German Idealism appeared within Judaism, substituting for the plan of history the *necessity* of his own (speculative) philosophical conclusions, that is, his own *system*. The necessity of the plan of history is apparent only to God. That is to say, it takes place by predestination, but allows man, with his finite capacity for knowledge, to be situated in the *freedom* of every decision.

In Formstecher, as also in Samuel Hirsch, we can see especially clearly that there can never be a possibility of true dialogue based on idealistic systematic philosophy, which, in the solitude of ratiocination, generates its concepts from within itself. Given the basis of a revelation acknowledged by faith, both Judaism and Christianity lay claim to a truth which cannot be made relative, for both cannot participate in it equally. From the idealistic perspective, the tension between them can never be seen, or even comprehended, as a reality. Compared to the efforts of that representative of the Enlightenment, Mendelssohn, who at least could still debate with Lavater, Formstecher's efforts must actually be termed a regression—but not a going back—to the Jewish Middle Ages in which the principles were not conceptual, but doctrinal. According to them, the relationship between Judaism and Christianity was not a "polar dualism within the world-soul" leading toward the final attainment of historical "undifferentiation" (i.e., the Messianic Age), but was a sharp antithesis between truth and error.

Before a new basis could be laid for better realization and comprehension of the phenomena of opposition and tension, there appeared once more, upon the terrain the nineteenth century epistemological problem, the old medieval dogmatic contrast between true and false doctrine. But this time it was already modified by a modern tendency: to understand the history of false doctrine as an amalgamation of contradictory tendencies within its development.

3   SALOMON LUDWIG STEINHEIM

Formstecher's conception undoubtedly contained an element of truth: the origin and development of Christianity represent an amalgamation of Jewish and pagan (Greek) elements. Salomon Ludwig Steinheim (1789-1866), in the four volumes of his important work *Die Offenbarung nach dem Lehrbegriff der Synagoge* ("Revelation according to the doctrine of the Synagogue") (1835-1865), used this idea as the pivotal point of an extremely acute polemic. The third volume of this, his life work, bears the subtitle *Der Kampf der Offenbarung mit dem Heidentum, ihre Synthese und Analyse* ("The Struggle of Revelation with Paganism, Their Synthesis and Analysis") (Leipzig, 1863). In it, Steinheim wrote from the Jewish point of view, a kind of polemic history of the Christian Church and doctrine. Unfortunately, it was quite unsystematic and random. The polemic is completely doctrinal in nature and thus, from the Jewish point of view, more legitimate than any of the more or less arbitrary distinctions resulting from speculative systematic philosophy.

With great emphasis (and, admittedly, with endless repetition), Steinheim took the field against "reduction of the Jewish religion to a philosophical system" through the identity principle of Formstecher and Schelling, or the ingenious mathematical philosophical conception of the idea-process, developed by Hirsch and Hegel (*Die Offenbarung nach dem Lehrbegriff der Synagoge,* II, 36 f.; III, 319; IV, 200, 240 f.; and *passim*). Of course, Steinheim's inferential argument is not at all suitable for furnishing a basis for religious dialogue. Nevertheless, in spite of all polemic exaggeration and his obvious blindness to the historical nature of the Jewish covenant community and his equally obvious bias on behalf of "pure doctrine," he produces *more* genuine Jewish theology than any other Jewish thinker of the nineteenth century. For this reason, S. L. Steinheim is an extremely important thinker and controversialist. He was almost the only nineteenth-century Jewish theologian (a physician, he called himself a "lay theologian") to hold fast to the central supernatural fact of revelation. This happened at a time when, except for the narrow circle of Orthodoxy, all basic doctrinal concepts had been reduced to the level of humanitarian ethics. His orthodox faith was perhaps more biblical than the greater part of the Christian Church and Christian theology of his day.

Beginning with his first appearance in the arena of philosophical theology (in 1833, writing in opposition to a philosopher of history, Heinrich Ritter, in Hengstenberg's *Evangelische Kirchenzeitung*), Steinheim raised one basic objection against the Christianity of the Church. It goes back to Lessing's distinction between the "religion of Christ" and the "Christian religion"; but in this case the distinction takes on a special meaning. In the religious history of all mankind—including Israel—he sees the conflict of two hostile, mutually exclusive, principles at work. The one is the pure principle of divine revelation, which has invaded history as something *totaliter aliter,* compelling human reason to recognition and faith even in spite of its actual intention. The other is the primitive human principle of mythophilosophy, which, within human history, has brought to light the aprioristic philosophical dogmas constructed by speculative reason in their manifold possibilities and variants. According to Steinheim, true revelation is invariably audible (precept and doctrine), not visible (incarnation). Thus its organ is the ear, while the eye is connected with covetousness. This distinction, which occurs also in Kierkegaard's work, probably goes back to Philo. The pure principle of the Jewish revelation— the belief in the unity of God, the creation of the world *ex nihilo,* and man's freedom (to fear God)—was also the real teaching of Christ, before it was distorted by human additions. For instance, the Gospel of Mark reports Jesus' reply to the question of the Pharisees asking which commandment was the most important: the reply was the Jewish confession of faith in the *unity* of God (Mark 12:28-30). This answer was already considerably altered and abbreviated in the accounts of Matthew and Luke. In the Gospel of John, which is completely non-Jewish (1:1-16), the first commandment is replaced by a mythological discourse upon the divine Trinity, in which Jesus himself appears as the second person of the Godhead; the origin of this could probably be seen in Egyptian and Syrian mystery cults. "Here (*sc.* in the Gospel of John) appear clearly both heterogeneous elements which, in combination, give rise to the basic dogma of Christianity: the doctrine of the concretely individual, self-conscious unity of revelation, and the pagan philosophical mysticism of Plato. On the one hand, by explicit concession and differentiation, the divine word gave us a creation *ex nihilo;* on the other, a dogma achieved by the operation of the mind, its basis within us. This latter dogma reappears in protean form in all systems of pagan theology, mysticism, and philosophy; it is usually called pantheism."[101]

This serious basic ambivalence (he continues), which is associated with the period of the origin of Christianity, has not vanished yet; fortunately, the Synagogue did not allow this same mythical manner of thought, contained in the writings of Alexandrian Judaism, to become of major importance in Palestine. The doctrinal system of the Church is put together out of philosophy and the doctrine of revelation (Steinheim, III, 77). What is actually wrong with this hybrid is that the true notion of creation of *omnia ex nihilo,* which basically contradicts the rational principle of *ex nihilo nihil fit,* is endangered by the doctrine of the Trinity, which was made binding in the time of Athanasius. Within the Godhead itself two uncreate persons were affirmed, and the pagan doctrine of predestination replaced freedom. In his role as a religious philosopher who has been influenced by the Enlightenment and Kant, Steinheim makes epistemological demands: he sees an epistemological contradition in the "doctrine of the Son" as an "equally substantial person, standing at once for a cosmic creative power and an historical person." (*Ibid.,* III, 100) "As *eternally-begotten Word,* he is the eternal cosmic divinity; as the child of a woman, born within time, he is telluric, finite, mortal: the *historical* Christ. But it is obvious that one and the same being cannot be both finite and infinite, temporal and eternal, but must be either the one or the other. Thus it is clear that we can no more unite the eternal cosmic principle with the historical Christ, the son of time, than we can think of a mystical Trinity in conjunction with the personal God." (*Ibid.,* III, 101)

This syncretism, developed upon the basis of an epistemological contradiction, according to the dictum *credo quia absurdum,* attained its full development only in the era of the Church Fathers, and was immortalized in the Nicene Creed and the *Quicunque vult.* In fact, however, it was latently present in the contrast between the Apostles Peter and Paul as the opposition of the Gentile Christians to the Jewish Christians. In defining the doctrine of the Trinity, the Nicene Creed worked out the exact nature of the amalgam. In this hybrid dogma, pieces of doctrine from both Judaism and paganism "were shaken together and united into a homogeneous mixture with amazing intellectual power, but also with a capriciousness which is almost terrifying. (*Ibid.,* III, 243) All subsequent Church history flows out of the continuing dualism of Jewish and pagan elements within the unifying formula. "The *content* of the continuing development of Christianity down to the present day is the alternation between both these doctrines of God, which had been fused into one, now tending toward the unity doctrine of revelation, now toward the plurality doctrine of paganism and philosophy." (*Isr. Volkslehrer,* 1860, p. 92) According to Steinheim, the "Jewish" protest of many sects within the Church was directed against the pagan corruption of the basic doctrine of genuine revelation, unity of God, creation, and freedom, throughout the history of paganism. He gives a copious catalogue of these sects, from the Ebionites through the Arians, Pelagians, Molinists, Socinians, and so forth, down to the modern Unitarians of all varieties.

Surely Steinheim is not so far wrong in his view that the history of Christianity down to the immediate present is shot through with a struggle between Jewish elements of revelation, on the one hand, and pagan myths and *philosophemata,* which always threaten to dominate. It takes only a slight change to convert the Christian doctrine of the Trinity into the Hegelian triad of the idea-process, or a creed of the religion of nature (being—becoming—decay); to convert the doctrine of creation into a doctrine of emanation, explaining material objects or organisms as eternally existent, emanated by God, thereby mythically divinizing them; or, finally, to allow man's freedom of action and moral responsibility to be erased from the doctrine of freedom as a consequence of an improper view of the world, emphasizing the preponderance of deterministic elements (Augustinian and Lutheran predestination), removing the claim of the divine imperative upon the individual addressed. Thus both the comprehensibility of the divine law and the possibility of ethical conduct are abolished together.

It is common knowledge that the Christian Church has continually been subject to these dangers, and is still subject to them. But Steinheim is wrong to assert that, as a consequence of the post-Nicene pagan-Jewish amalgamation, this *must* be so. All the effort of the Church—particularly within Protestantism—strives to avoid this danger, and is able to avoid it, through ever-renewed enunciation of correct belief, as well as through correct doctrinal definition. Partial as his vision was, unsystematic and unhistorical as his thought was, Steinheim's voice should be attended to by true Christians as a warning. It was he who undertook, in the very midst of the nineteenth century, to remain at his post as an Israelite, "as a member of that great missionary body which for thousands of years here below has been honored not so much with thanklessness as with defamation and death." (*Vom Bleibenden und Vergänglichen im Judentum,* p. 30) His theology tended to seek a way of drawing the "religion of Christ" into the realm of the Jewish faith. He expressly states the purpose of this effort, *the* goal of his controversial theology, in the foreword to the second volume of his *Offenbarungslehre* (1856), pp. xii f.: "Let the false watchmen of Zion, who have given hospitable welcome to paganism, not always unintentionally, rejecting from their midst the word of revelation; let all of those who have counterfeited our pure concept of revelation, adulterating it with pagan philosophical elements, chide as an *enemy of Christianity* the man who has accused them of neglecting their duty and being unfaithful in their stewardship of their precious talent. He will not shrink back on that account, but, rather, accept this title if they speak of their own mixture and call it a kind of Christianity. I cannot so designate it. A Christianity which is not independently based as much upon revelation pure and simple as upon myth and philosophy is not worthy of the name! It may be a good philosophy, a myth laden with significance, a pleasant emotional religion—I have nothing against these. Only let it not be called *revelation* and the teaching of Christ, but the very opposite—apostasy from it. It leads to the gods of Merus and Mt. Olympus, not to him who revealed himself to Moses upon Sinai, who instructed the Christ and the Apostle to the Gentiles. The critique of revelation is that it leads to him and to the knowledge of his nature and will, insofar as it has pleased him to illuminate and correct our reason in these matters. That man would show himself a true friend and promoter of the *religion of Christ* whom these others would view, justifiably, as the enemy of *their* Christian belief. But that is the doctrine of the unity of God, the freedom of man, and the creation of the world. Upon these three pillars, and upon them alone, rests and must rest every revealed religion, including the religion of Christ, if it is to retain the name of revealed religion."

To Salomon Ludwig Steinheim must go the credit for fighting a lonely battle in the nineteenth century. He proclaimed once more the lost and forgotten fact that in the revealed religion of God, the first and foremost consideration is *truth*. Judaism, too, cannot do without dogmatic formulations if it wishes to define itself, to differentiate itself clearly and consciously from other religious creeds and from false doctrines within itself. On the basis of his postulates, Steinheim was not able to promote the cause of Judaeo-Christian dialogue. Nevertheless, through preliminary elucidation and definition, he contributed to the fashioning of a true *basis* for dialogue, striving against liberal obliteration of boundaries and the reduction of religion to philosophy.

VII
EXISTENTIAL
RELIGIOUS DIALOGUES

For nineteen centuries, Jews and Christians have passed through the world beside each other. There has been no lack of side glances, but true dialogue never developed—nor, in fact, could it develop. During the first centuries, the Jewish side had no other interest than refuting Christian reinterpretations of Jewish doctrines, holding themselves aloof from true encounter through "refutations" of their opponent. When Christianity acceded to power, Christians no longer had any serious *desire* to engage in discussion with the Jews, for the latter's very impotence was seen as an overwhelming instance of God's punishment. Within the intellectual arena of medieval scholasticism, Jews and Christians could properly have only the concern, of justifying their own religion, while at the same time flatly refusing to acknowledge the other's claim to truth. In the modern era, presuppositions changed. The first real discussion of modern times was already being carried on within the framework of a *new religion:* the religion of the Enlightenment. In spite of his traditional manner of life, Moses Mendelssohn (according to Steinheim's rather too subtle rebuke) retained not much more of the *doctrinal* faith of Judaism than "forms without content, age-old accustomed ceremonies, wigs, and beards." Seventy years later, in the era of the great philosophical systems, Formstecher and Hirsch erected great Jewish religious philosophies, which included Christianity within the framework of their speculative views. The concern then was once more with doctrine, but the doctrinal content of both religions was, in both senses, lost in speculation. Steinheim's "orthodox" protest probably helped restore the structure of Jewish religious doctrine, though admittedly neglecting the problems connected with the law. But the real concern of Christianity remained uncomprehended.

In the course of the nineteenth century, political and religious liberalism prevailed to an ever greater degree. At the same time, conditions continued to develop under which real encounter could take place. For real encounter can become possible only within the realm of freedom, in which all participants in the conversation are allowed openly to declare the truth to which they bear witness, without the constant fear that thereby they may suffer personal harm, or encounter invincible prejudices on the part of the other side from the outset. Only within this atmosphere of external freedom can that inner freedom develop which is able to ask questions and allow questions to be asked in complete openness. Under these circumstances, in expressing its own point of view, it can take seriously the concern of the other, understanding itself from the other's point of view, without at the same time relativizing the position of either. Such real understanding seeks neither to confuse nor to confound; it is well aware of its own limits, but conducts a real dialogue *within* these limits. Only in the twentieth century has such an understanding become truly possible. It has brought about results which are of importance and will remain significant within the secular world. In many places today this precious possession of liberality threatens along with the gift of speech itself, to be lost once more; but, in spite of such threat, it is perhaps the only real "progress" vis-à-vis the Middle Ages of which the twentieth century can boast. It would be, however, a serious misunderstanding of this recognized fact were the progress interpreted to consist in an "abolition of dogma." In such a case it would not be progress, but disintegration. Its fruitfulness lies rather in the fact that the speaker of today undertakes to conduct a dialogue with all his heart. That is, he dares to involve *himself* in the discussion, not nominalistically, that is, through the expression of *nomina*, but realistically assuming responsibility for the dialogue, for allowing the *nomina* to become *realia* in and through the witness of the individual. This is the true progress vis-à-vis the religious debates of the Middle Ages. Whereas in the medieval disputations the delegates of Judaism and Christianity delivered monologues in a "discussion," the outcome of which was already determined before it had begun, in the real dialogue of the modern era, something basically new has occurred— the "opponent" has become a "partner"; the "monologue," a "dialogue"; creedal dogmas are not expounded but must be vindicated through the life of the speaker. A dialogue thus vindicated, asking meaningful questions and giving meaningful answers, establishes a *communicating body,* so that the participants and any listeners who happen to be present are drawn into the conversation in such a way that *within* it they become a corporate body. When such a conversation is properly conducted, conflicting beliefs are not abolished. Instead, the conflicts arising from what is acknowledged through faith are brought into sharp relief; but there is real understanding in a third realm, that of spirit and truth, from which religion developed.

Such dialogues between Jews and Christians have been conducted several times in the twentieth century.[102] As the most outstanding, we shall present here the conversations between Franz Rosenzweig and Eugen Rosenstock-Huessy, and between Martin Buber and Karl Ludwig Schmidt. But the mere mention of these names brings up a suspicion which must be dealt with first. These men bear ordinary doctoral and professorial titles. Can they, then, speak as legitimately for their group as did the speakers in the academies of the first centuries, or the rabbinic exegetes of the Middle Ages, the Church Fathers, and the Schoolmen? What is to prevent us from coming up with groundless innovations of modern minds, altogether liable to whim and change? In actual fact, there is nothing to protect us. The twentieth century has seen the disintegration of the traditional spheres of life and doctrine from which, formerly, authorized representatives spoke. Ultimately, authorization to speak is relegated completely to the subjectivity of the speaker. Today no conclusions can be drawn concerning the Christian or Jewish quality of the life of a representative of the Christian or Jewish community on the basis of his office. Therefore, there can be no other authorization, no other warrant, than that which emerges from the life of the speaker and bespoken by the doctrinal content of his life.

A Jew and a Christian conduct a Judaeo-Christian dialogue only when the contrasting beliefs of the centuries are brought to bear in their conversation, when their questions have their environment and setting within, with the consequence that the breakup of old questions in the present day implies that an organic life juncture is being made with historical tradition. In the process, the solidified mass of tradition gives way, opens up to the future, and continues on through the new conversation. What has been worked out on the basis of individual questions and in the forms of present-day thinking receives objective corroboration, and thus legitimation, in the knowledge of the centuries. The new conversation joins itself, by virtue of its content and its comparisons, to the tradition of conversations which have already taken place. There will be modern Judaeo-Christian conversations, new formulations of the questions, individual ways of contemplating the phenomena; but in them we shall find the *same* conflicts of belief—Christian statements and Jewish replies—which we have exhibited from the Talmudic and Midrashic documents of the first centuries. We can even go so far as to say that it is only the fact that these same conflicts—even though refracted and diffused by the prism of history—can be found again in the conversations of today, which legitimates the speakers, providing the evidence that their conversation, conducted on their own responsibility, has been conducted essentially as a Judaeo-Christian dialogue. It is thus that through two persons, without office and without external authority, Israel and Christianity join in debate, or continue the debate which has already lasted more than nineteen hundred years.

1   FRANZ ROSENZWEIG—
    EUGEN ROSENSTOCK-HUESSY

These are the possibilities for genuine dialogue which the twentieth century has opened to our generation. Given their basis it follows that we no longer have to proceed as in the previous chapter, by referring to systematic works such as

Formstecher's *Religion des Geistes* or Steinheim's *Offenbarung,* but are able, instead, to exhibit the tension between Judaism and Christianity within the framework of a genuine dialogue which *actually* took place.

In the summer of 1913, a year before the outbreak of the Great War, three intellectually passionate young men were together in Leipzig: Eugen Rosenstock-Huessy (born 1888), who was subsequently to hold a chair in German legal history at Breslau; Rudolf Ehrenberg (born 1889), at that time lecturer in medicine at Göttingen; and the latter's second cousin, Franz Rosenzweig (1886-1929). Rosenzweig stands beside Martin Buber (together with whom he undertook a German translation of Scripture) as the religious thinker and active believer who attained the greatest intellectual significance for German Judaism of the twentieth century. The immediate outcome of the conversations of that summer in Leipzig was two letters, written in summary by Franz Rosenzweig to Rudolf Ehrenberg (dated October 20 and November 4, 1913), as well as twenty-one letters exchanged between Eugen Rosenstock-Huessy and Franz Rosenzweig, which continued to develop the theme of the discussion. These latter, written three years later, between May and December of 1916, were exchanged between the Macedonian and the French fronts, from foxhole to foxhole.[103] These letters paved the way for large portions of Rosenzweig's systematic treatise *Der Stern der Erlösung,* ("The Star of Redemption") likewise conceived at this time, which also discusses the questions relevant here. With the inclusion of many political and philosophical questions of the past and present, these letters discuss ultimate matters of religion with an abundance and vibrancy of thought which can scarcely be found in any analogous exchange of letters. This dialogistic correspondence may be put forward as the purest form of Judaeo-Christian dialogue ever attained, perhaps even for ages to come. The foxhole letters exchanged by Rosenzweig and Rosenstock-Huessy refer back to their religious discussions in Leipzig, which were intended to answer Rosenzweig's question whether he should convert to Christianity or remain a Jew—or, more correctly, *become* a Jew.

2 THE MEANING OF ISRAEL FOR CHRISTIANITY

In what follows, we shall for the most part permit the men and their letters to speak for themselves rather than to discuss them ourselves, as has been appropriate up to now. But the style of the "new thought" demands also a change in the style of presentation. Rosenzweig himself prescribes this, writing in one of these letters: "It is perhaps unnecessary to say anything at all *about* that which is living; one must only await the moment in which itself it expresses itself." (*Briefe*, p. 712) Properly understood, these "formal" expressions are themselves "material," as will now be shown. In the midst of this epistolary discussion, we shall see once more the ancient doubts and questions, raised anew under the prompting of "historical facts," which must be correctly understood in order that the *new* insight be apprehended.

Rosenstock-Huessy formulates as follows the first basic question, often discussed, of the meaning which Israel has for Christianity: "You are the human individual, whose individuality I acknowledge in spite of his non-Christian character. The Jews are as much the chosen people and the Old Testament as much the law of the *fathers* as the New is the love of the children, so that of course the Church needs 'its' Jews to guarantee its own veracity. Jewish hardness of heart is, so to speak, a Christian dogma. But is it also, can it be also a Jewish doctrine? That is the trench; I do not see how you can capture it." (*Ibid.,* p. 663)

The thoughtful answer given by Rosenzweig to this direct question has many levels, for the same ideas keep reappearing at different junctures and continually intersect one another. For the purposes of our presentation, they must be detached laboriously and often violently from the living body of several different contexts in the letters. First, Rosenzweig's answer refers to "historical relationships"—why it was necessary that Paul's "personal theory" of the simultaneous election and rejection of the Jews, as well as the inner connection between the law and the Gospel of the Church, should cease to be a personal theory and become a fixed dogma of tradition. This happened only because the heretic Marcion, with his conception of the destruction of the old god, foreign to the new age, wanted to draw the conclusion (based on Pauline teaching) of a one-sided rejection—the Jews as children of the devil. The Church *had* to hold fast to the identification of the creator-god, who had also spoken through Moses and the prophets, with the Father of Jesus Christ, establishing this identity dogmatically. Thus was laid down the historical connection with the Jews, but at the same time the end of their historical role, which would regain meaning once more only at the end of history as the "enlightenment of the hard of heart." "But," writes Rosenzweig in his account to Ehrenberg of the Leipzig dispute, revealing *in nuce* a whole "system" of Jewish historical theology, "the Church does not see *why* it is confronted by a point of absolute hardness of heart in the world (this 'why' is a mystery to it), it knows only *that* it is so." (*Ibid.,* p. 78) On the basis of this circumstance, Franz Rosenzweig explains the ancient and modern misconceptions and attacks of the Church. He joins the traditional line of discussion at three focal points, examining the ancient conflict of faith (which secretly is an agreement) in modern language and on the basis of experiences of the present day: (1) The Church has reinterpreted the "hardness of heart" of the Jews so that it means "rejection by God." But the Jew feels this "hardness of heart" as "faithfulness." Real rebellion against God, which is not rejection, but rebellion, can be made good only by *teshûbhah,* not metanoia; by return, not by repentance. The Septuagint, translating a word under conditions of a different faith-experience, falsified and *had* to falsify the original meaning, with this translation: "The history of the world rests in the dictionary."[104] (2) Similarly, the wrath of God: this did not begin with the Exile, but follows directly from election, as its complement. "We ascribe perfect devotion, not to the history of the nation, but to the age of the patriarchs; it is only to this that we 'appeal' in the presence of God." (3) The year 70 constitutes a caesura in the sense that after that, apocalyptic restoration is awaited concretely. "Henceforth we are compelled no longer to hope for individual reconciliation after individual apostasy, but only the great reconciliation of the Last Day. Previously, single prophets came at singular times; but since that date we await no more prophets, but only the prophet on the Last Day." (*Ibid.,* p. 78)

In this discussion, the questions have not been quoted in detail, but they can be derived from the content of the answers. We see that the ancient themes have been taken up once more, although Rosenzweig's statements and formulations, made on the basis of present-day historical consciousness, have a somewhat different ring than the homilies of the Midrashic teachers of the first centuries. But the decisive thing in either case is the inner connection between Jewish historical impotence, as a fact of history demonstrated by events—interpreted by Christians as "rejection" (the effect of this theologoumenon being anti-Semitism), by Jews as "punishment"—and the *election,* as the second "historical fact," reported in the Bible and acknowledged in faith by the Jewish self-awareness of the centuries. The doctrine of "election" is another point of separation between the thinkers. In his letter, Rosenstock-Huessy had opposed the whole concept of a theological place accorded to a people or nation, since Christianity has *redeemed* the individual from family and nation, forming them all into a "new unity of all sinners, those who labor and are heavy laden." "Since A.D. 70, there are only peoples, and the chosen people has been reduced to the status of a mere chemical indicator for all nationalism." (*Ibid.,* p. 680) Today, late in the history of the West, the peoples having become the *orbis terrarum,* natural belief in God on the part of the nations has become the "old covenant without covenant and law." The special case of the nation of Israel *since* the appearance of Christ is an anachronism; their knowledge of themselves as a nation has become unreal and moribund. For the space of two thousand years, Israel, unlike Christianity, has been unable to alter the face of the earth. It has served only to furnish a few famous names to the glory of the Synagogue, nothing more.

"For two thousand years the Synagogue has spoken of what it possesses in possessing nothing at all; but it does not experience what it is, and will, therefore, never discover what it is. It illustrates the curse of self-assurance, of aristocratic pride and thoughtless indifference toward the evolutionary law of the unified cosmos, of 'peace on earth to all with whom he is pleased.' It does not know that new mankind of universal sin and need, the forever regenerate *corpus christianum* of all men of good will that is 'beyond all people.' It knows a causal togetherness of blood, of the chosen people, but no final 'belonging to each other' of all children of the Father. They possess the promise that one day all peoples will worship toward Jerusalem, and they continue to crucify the one who came to fulfill that promise. With all the strength at their command, they stand opposed to their own promise. Upon earth they represent Lucifer, the highest of the angels, elect of God, who finally wished to hold fast to God's gift to him as a power which was his by right—and fell. Thus Judah presumes upon its own inalienable right. This naïveté, which presumes to have won from God inalienable and immutable rights, which 'naturally' now continue for posterity through the inheritance of acquired characteristics—that is the blind antiquity of the Jews." (*Ibid.*, pp. 681 f.)

In his reply, Rosenzweig tries to deal with the multitude of problems lying behind these few sentences. His answers are not systematic explanations, but unsystematic and spontaneous formulations. His first concern, as a basic clarification of the situation, is to separate the election of the people of Israel from the phenomena of modern nationalism and "national" faith. This election is something different in kind from a natural feeling of election, such as is a part of very modern nationalism.

"Thus even now, when election has become an indicator of every nationalism, the election of the Jews is something peculiar, because it is the election of the 'One Nation.' Here arrogance or modesty, the hate of others or the scorn of others, even empirical comparison with other nations, lose their meaning. The concept has lost none of its metaphysical weight, although its content (to it, atavism was only a symbol; messianism alone was the content) now has become common property. For it is still (and will always remain) the unique, *visibly real* incarnation of the *attained* goal of unity (of the 'one people upon earth,' as it calls itself in the Sabbath prayer), while the nations are only upon the road toward this goal, which is yet to be reached; so they must be, if it is ever really to be attained. The Jewish idea of election, from the beginning, is anything but 'naïve.' Were it naïve, i.e., atavistic, then anti-Semitism would be inexplicable; for there is honor among thieves. But it was at *Sinai* (not at the grove of Mamre), says an old punning legend, that Israel gained the *śinnâh,* the hate of the peoples. The Jews are the only non-naïve nation of the ancient world, for the Jewish concept of election discovers its 'origin' only when it has experienced its 'destiny.'" (*Ibid.,* p. 687)

In *Der Stern der Erlösung,* Rosenzweig described these correlations at great length. Israel *is* at the goal; the nations are still upon the road. Therefore, they hate Israel, and yet know that it is indispensable for mankind. But in the exchange of letters, the point has been reached where nothing more can be clarified in order to correct Christian statements "apologetically":

"But now I note, as I try to continue writing, that everything I should now have to write to you is beyond my power to express to you. For I should now have to be able to show Judaism to you from within, hymnically, just as you should have to show Christianity to me, an outsider. For the same reason that you cannot do this, neither can I. The soul of Christianity is in its expressions; while to the world outside, Judaism shows only its hard, protective shell; only within can one speak of its soul. And so it simply will not work, and you shall have to trust me when I say that the so-to-speak abstract content of devotion among you and among us is one and the same." (*Ibid.,* p. 688)

But now where does the difference really lie? In the previous letter, Rosenstock-Huessy had drawn a parallel between

the sacrifice of Abraham and that of Agamemnon. Thus he
assimilated Judaism too much to ancient pagan conceptions,
instead of drawing the proper comparison: that between
Abraham's sacrifice and the sacrificial act of Christ. For this
reason, in continuing the correspondence, Rosenzweig uses
this as the point of attack in order to see the essential difference between Israel and Christianity as the difference between Moriah and Golgotha.

"You have confused Abraham and Agamemnon. The
latter, it is true, sacrificed what he *had* for the sake of another
—what he wanted, or, if you like, what it was his duty to
want. In fact, he himself did not even perform the sacrifice,
but only delivered it over, and then stood by with veiled head.
But Abraham did not sacrifice *something,* not *a* child, but his
'only' son, and, what is more, the son of the promise. He sacrifices this son to the God who made the promise (the traditional Jewish commentaries even read this paradox into the
text); and through this sacrifice, in the eyes of man, the content of the promise becomes impossible. It is not for nothing
that this pericope is assigned to our highest holy days. It is
the prototypical sacrifice, not of personal identity (Golgotha), but of national existence, of the 'son' and all future
sons (for we appeal before God to this sacrifice, or, rather, to
this readiness to sacrifice; specifically that of the father, not
that of the son, though the latter is emphasized in the narra-
tive).[105] The son is given back: henceforth he is *only* a son
of promise. Nothing more happens, no Ilium falls, the
promise merely remains in force; it was not for the sake of
some Ilium that the father was ready to sacrifice, but 'without cause.' *Agamemnon* sacrifices something 'that he has,'
but *Abraham,* everything that he could be; *Christ,* everything that he is. That, as you write, is really 'the whole difference.' To the 'naïvely' stated, inalienable claim upon God,

there corresponds something you have forgotten: the equally 'naïvely' assumed yoke of inalienable suffering, which we know—'naïvely?'—has been laid upon us. (Traditional commentary on Isa. 53): 'For the redemption of the world' (—'Lucifer'?? Kindly be a little more sparing with your symbols!—). And yet we do not strive toward this redemption, *which will also be our redemption from 'suffering.'* On the contrary: to the holy unrest of our labor there corresponds, in our case, the holy anxiety lest redemption come 'before its time' (in reference to which there exist the strangest, downright grotesque, legends, ancient and modern), an anxiety which forms the metaphysical basis of our attitude toward Christianity, just as that unrest forms the basis of your attitude toward Judaism." (*Ibid.*, p. 689)

Thus the sacrifice of Abraham is prototypical for Israel, establishing concretely and corporeally the special status of the Jews before God and man. Quite in accord with tradition, it is viewed as the origin of the election and the promise; these, according to the gracious promise of the Lord, remain bound to the physical seed of Abraham. This is different from the way in which access is opened to the pagan through Christ's sacrifice of the New Covenant. Instead, since it pleased God to accept Abraham's readiness to sacrifice, as son of God, Israel has always been (through the law) in real union with God, or, rather, has as an inheritance the latent possibility of the union. In a later letter, dated October 2, 1917, Rosenzweig elucidates this immensely important situation once more. It arises from the fact that in Judaism the *nation* is the vehicle of revelation, and childbearing is a sacred duty. "It is precisely through the fact of its once-and-for-all character, strongly emphasized by tradition, that the sacrifice of Isaac has eternal significance for us. No Jew can relinquish his son, the son of promise; Abraham's renunciation took place *on behalf of* all generations to come, so that thenceforth no one should have to imitate it. Just as the death on the cross took place for all Christians yet to come, so that they might live." (*Ibid.*, p. 248) "Blood-relationship" is not counted holy for its own sake; every precaution is taken to preserve it because of the *promise,* so that the individual born a Jew can exalt physical calling into the sphere of metaphysical election (the yoke of the kingdom of heaven)—"on account of the *messianic* goal." At the "end of days," all mankind will be "as proselytes." "The living devotion of popular prayer" knows almost nothing of "worship in *Jerusalem,*" but only of "worshiping God alone" and "uniting in One Covenant." (*Ibid.*, p. 693) This means that Judaism confesses a *universal* God and a *universal* will of God as well as a *universal* goal of man; but it cannot go its way through history as a missionary religion—on account of the covenant between the One God and the One People, to which will be added, at the end of time, One Mankind.

In his answer, Rosenzweig had already discussed the nature and significance of "nationhood for the Jewish religion," in contrast to the nationalism of the nations of the world. Now his partner in the discussion puts the so-to-speak "internal" question: how he would evaluate this difference, surely sensible, in connection with *Zionism,* which beyond doubt takes a different view of the situation, and just in this circumstance typifies modern Judaism's view of itself: "Do you believe that Zionism is an accident?" (*Ibid.*, p. 695) Rosenzweig replies that within Judaism, Zionism represents an "emancipated form of the messianic movement." Thus it can gain influence in the minds of the Jews, even touching the depths of their Jewish existence, without being capable of altering them or their ideas: "It belongs completely to the series of messianic movements which have continuously existed within Judaism, more or less noble self-deceptions, attempts to take heaven by storm, 'now in our own day,' necessary for the preservation of the (inner) vitality of a nation cut off (exiled!) from the life of the world. . . . But if you had more knowledge of the Zionist movement than you have reason to, you would know that the inner (self-conscious) history of Zionism is the growing awareness of its ultimately *unimportant* importance." (*Ibid.*, p. 708) For Israel is not a nation like the nations which are along the way; by destiny it is already at the end of all ways, at the *goal,* when it assumes the yoke of the kingdom of heaven. The law of the Jews is not a bridge to God—simply incomprehensible, if understood from the standpoint of the Christian concept of a mediator—but a school of holiness, which has nothing to do either with righteousness or with concepts of merit. Instead, it causes him who follows it to be hallowed (not holy!) in the process. Being at the goal is the future *fulfillment* of the law; the Jews' *following* of it mediates to them a presentiment of the world to come, at the same time making them alert to the danger of false mediations and settlements within the course of history. But in this aeon, Israel must pay a price for this *immediate* walking in the light of God's countenance: "subjectively, through the misery of consciousness of being excluded, being peculiar; and objectively, through the fact that to you we are the monument which warns you continually of your *not-yet.* You who live in an *ecclesia triumphans* have need of a dumb servant, which, when you think you *already enjoy* God in the bread and the wind, may cry out to you: Master, be mindful of the last things!" (*Ibid.*, p. 690)

3 THE MEANING OF CHRISTIANITY FOR ISRAEL

Concomitant with the peculiar character of this discussion is the fact that the nature of one's own faith must always be discussed when the meaning of the other's faith for it is under discussion. In Rosenstock-Huessy's case, when he discusses the rejection of the Jews, he must also speak of Christian dogma; and, in order to explain the meaning of Christianity for Israel, Rosenzweig must say something of the nature of Judaism—as much as is "expressible." What is new in such interrelationships is this: they derive from the modern historical conciousness, and possess a breadth of vision and depth of insight which differ from all the toleration of the Enlightenment. For Rosenzweig is aware of the modern possibility of knowing upon reflection that there is an *external* view of, knowledge about, and judgment upon an alien phenomenon, based upon one's own standpoint of belief; but there must *also* be a seeing, knowing, and judging from *within,* which the other possesses only in his own right. It may be communicable, but cannot be taken over and utilized by anyone else—at most, it can be accepted only on the level of information. Franz Rosenzweig now makes use of this method (which penetrates deeply) for Judaeo-Christian dialogue, for determining the actual points of conflict, with great success. Admittedly, he goes too far, extending this new method of thought also backward into the past, sharpening it to the statement that Christianity, as a force which fills the world, has always been Jewish dogma. Although this cannot be demonstrated on the basis of traditional formulations (naturally he alludes to Judah ha-Levi's metaphor of the tree as a support for his statement), and therefore it does not belong in the "substantial class of dogmas"; it is *only* a "theologoumenon," but can be derived from "an analysis of the consciousness of the believer." (*Ibid.,* p. 670) In this regard, there is much important material in the letters to Rudolf Ehrenberg, which once more take up Formstecher's missionary idea (which Rosenzweig can hardly have known of) in *historical* form, namely, from the viewpoint of the twentieth century.

"*Our* recognition of Christianity rests, in fact, upon Christianity, namely upon the fact that Christianity recognizes *us*. It is the Torah, ultimately, which is spread abroad by Bible societies to the most distant islands. Any Jew would have to admit this. Of course, the Jewish consciousness does not base itself upon the relationship of the Christian Church to the world; it merely finds itself once more in that situation. Per se, it knows nothing of this: Isaiah 55:5. Therefore, it needs no new revelation within history; the events of the first century have not changed its task, only its historical destiny. Since then, the situation is new, and, as I believe, definitive for the rest of time. But only the *situation*; the Mishnah, the work in which Judaism at that time constructed for itself a new basis, seeks to be only a 'repetition' (the meaning of *Mishnah*) of the Torah; the entire Talmud serves as proof that this was really the case." (*Ibid.*, p. 77)

This postulate of genuine *recognition* takes in good faith the faith of someone else—is itself, so to speak, a "faith in the dative." Only as a result of this could Rosenzweig, on the basis of historical self-understanding, proceed in the third book of *Der Stern der Erlösung* to give a presentation of everything *Christian* in its historical manifestations. In spite of its positive insight and substantial character, which will probably hardly ever be surpassed by a Jew, it is almost completely unknown. And yet it is of enormous, inexhaustible importance, not only for the phenomenology of religion. Starting from this recognition of the other faith in its own depth of belief, Rosenzweig can even admit what no Jew before him ever admitted of his own free will—and without this Jewish admission, in the future, no further discussion is possible—that not one of the nations of the world comes to the Father except through Jesus Christ.

"What Christ and his Church mean within the world—on this point we are agreed. No one comes to the Father except through him. No one *comes* to the Father—but the situation is different when one need no longer come to the Father because he *is* already with him. That is the case with the nation of Israel (not the individual Jew). The development of Judaism passes by Jesus, to whom the heathen say 'Lord,' and through whom they 'come to the Father'; it does not pass through him. (It remains open to discuss Rabbi Jeshua, the Nazarene, and the possibility that—as 'rabbi,' not as 'Lord,'—he could experience a renaissance among us modern Jews. In any case, that would not be of decisive importance.) The nation of Israel, elected by its Father, keeps its gaze fixed beyond world and history toward that last, most distant, point where he, Israel's Father, will himself be the one and only—'all in all'! At this point, where Christ ceases to be Lord, Israel ceases to be elect. On this day, God loses the name by which Israel alone may call upon him; God is then no longer 'Israel's' God. But until this time it is Israel's life to anticipate this eternal day in confession of faith and in action, to stand as a living symbol of this day, a nation of priests with the law, to hallow the name of God through its own holiness. The condition of this people of God within the world, the external (persecution) and internal (hardness of heart) misery it assumes by virtue of its separation—upon this, too, we are agreed.

"Nevertheless, since the Synagogue assumed these miseries resulting from denial of the world in the same ultimate hope as the Church assumes the miseries resulting from affirmation of the world, and since this is not merely an unconscious and accidental rendezvous in *eternity* (such as that between the faithful and the 'universal' pacifists), but, in addition, the roots of this hope, the God of all *time,* both now and then, rise up together, the revelation of the Old Covenant is common to us both: thus are Church and Synagogue referred to each other.

"The Synagogue, immortal, but with broken staff and eyes covered, must renounce all striving within the world, using all its strength to keep itself alive and pure from life. It relinquishes to the Church the universal mission (work of the world), recognizing in it salvation for the heathen throughout history. The Synagogue knows that what works of the cult achieve for Israel is achieved for the world outside Israel by works of love. But the Synagogue refuses to grant to the Church that the power by virtue of which the Church performs works of love is more than *divine,* being itself a power of God. In this, it fixes its gaze upon the future.

"And the Church, with unbreakable staff, eyes open to the world, warrior assured of victory, is forever in danger that those whom she conquers will dictate her laws. Sympathetic to all, she must, nevertheless, never lose herself in generalities. Her word forever must remain a foolishness and a stumbling block. The Greeks see to it that it may remain a foolishness, then as now, and in the future. They will always continue to ask why just *this* word should be a power of God, and this or that other word not be equally good—why Jesus and not (or, not also) Goethe. And their question will continue to the last day. Only it will become fainter and fainter, quieter and quieter, with the external or internal victory of the Church. For wisdom which thinks itself wise falls silent before the appearance of truth. And when the last Greek has been put to silence through the operation of the Church, then the word of the cross—at the *end* of time, but yet *within* time—will be foolishness to no one. But it will remain an everlasting stumbling block even at that moment. It would not be a stumbling block to a Greek to recognize a power of God in the world. The Greeks saw the world full of gods. One thing only was inexplicable to him: that he should worship just the one Saviour on the cross; so it is today, and shall be in the future. But the Synagogue had her eyes blindfolded: she saw no world—how, then, could she have seen gods in it? She saw only with the interior eye of the prophet, seeing thus only what was last and most distant. And thus it became a stumbling block to her, the demand that she see what was closest, something in the present, in the same way she saw only what was most distant; so it is today, and shall be in the future. Thus whenever the Church forgets that she is a stumbling block, and would gladly adjust herself to 'the human condition,' an action which would have been most welcome to the Greeks, who, like that Emperor, would gladly have set up a statue to Christ in their pantheon—when this happens, the Church finds in the Synagogue the dumb admonisher who, not enticed by the human condition, sees only the stumbling block. Then it becomes aware once more of its positive message, and speaks again the word of the cross. Thus the Church knows that Israel will be preserved until the day when the last Greek has perished, the work of love is completed, and the last day, the day of the harvest of hope, dawns." (*Ibid.*, pp. 73-75)

Thus defining the meaning of Christianity for Israel and—in mutual historical interpenetration of vocation and destiny—the meaning of Israel for Christianity, in these letters of 1913, Franz Rosenzweig—without "feeling any more at home in Christianity"—brought to light insights of astounding profundity and fundamental importance for future discussions. More than any other similar attempt, this will continue to be suitable for making radically comprehensible the mysterious conflict and alliance between Israel and Christianity. In *this* form, this affirmation of the divine origin of Christianity represents something basically novel for Judaism, transcending all traditional points of attack; it is of extreme fundamental importance. Here, reflection upon historical experience is united positively, i.e., following the organic development of tradition, with Jewish doctrinal content. Thus Eugen Rosenstock-Huessy draws an "ecclesiastical" conclusion from Jewish "hardness of heart," or, rather, abolishes the ancient conclusion, likewise on the basis of historical consciousness. He writes to his "opponent": "*No, the hardness of heart of the Jews is today no longer a Christian dogma.* Christ now has enough to crucify him within his Church. It is not true that today the Jews alone would crucify him, the Jews alone the world over." (*Ibid.,* p. 696)[106] For his own part, Franz Rosenzweig demands a further "ecclesiastical" conclusion based on the same historical consciousness. Concerning the question of a possible Evangelical mission to the Jews, he writes in a letter of January 1, 1926, to another cousin, Pastor Hans Ehrenberg: "Quite apart from the personal qualities of von Harling [*sc.* the respected leader of the German mission to the Jews]—the mission to the Jews is the true shibboleth which determines whether a person has grasped the true situation. There will continue to be some Jews baptized, even if the pastors make it as difficult as possible for those who come to them, but there must not be an organized mission to the Jews. That is the ecclesiastical point of *Der Stern der Erlösung.* The Jewish Christians have their justification, historically, in primitive Christianity, where they soon died out as the Gentile Church of Paul grew, and dogmatically, in Christian eschatology. In the meantime, in regard to the former, they are an anachronism; in regard to the latter, a paradox." (*Ibid.,* pp. 552 f.)

4 MARTIN BUBER—KARL LUDWIG SCHMIDT

The second religious dialogue of the present era, once more letting both participants state for themselves the essential part of their message, took place in 1933, between Martin Buber and the evangelical theologian Karl Ludwig Schmidt, under the auspices of the Jewish Academy in Stuttgart.[107] A similar statement on the part of Buber, which we shall draw upon for comparison, had been made three years previously in the same place, on the occasion of a "study-convention of the four German-language missionary societies concerned with the mission to the Jews."[108] Buber's discussion, for many years sophisticated and matured by his reflection on the nature of the "creature," is borne forward and interwoven with the dialogue-impulse characteristic of modern thought: it effaces nothing and refuses to gloss over differences, but, rather, contrasts with each other quite objectively "the Church's view of Israel and Israel's view of itself, in a manner which is more rigorous in its opposition than a merely logical contrasting." (*Die Stunde und die Erkenntnis,* p. 149: "The Time and the Perception.") Again the new basis of present-day religious debate becomes clear when we hear Buber formulate his answer, in full knowledge of what he is demanding of himself and of the other: "We can attempt something very difficult to do, something very difficult for the man with religious ties, something which strains against his ties and relationships, or, rather, seems to strain against them, something which seems to strain against his relationship with God—we can acknowledge, as a mystery, what someone else confesses as *his* faith-reality, contrary to our own existence, contrary to our knowledge of our own being. We are not capable of judging its meaning, because we do not know it from within as we know *ourselves* from within." (*Ibid.,* p. 152)

The administration of the Academy had stated as the theme for the debate: "Church, State, Nationhood, Judaism" —"concepts," as Karl Ludwig Schmidt, the first speaker, establishes at the outset, "which cannot be discussed abstractly, but only concretely and historically, in the sense of an event which has taken place and continues to repeat itself." Thus it is hardly accidental that Schmidt, also, formulates with his own words the central questions of tradition—hardly aware of its full extent—which have ever been the concern of Judaeo-Christian debate. It is no accident, because ultimately these questions must arise of their own accord out of every serious and honest examination of the objective phenomena. Schmidt mentions the messiahship of Jesus of Nazareth, the question of the election and rejection of Israel, the fact of the Diaspora (*gâlûth*), and the derivative question of Israel's position within the world; that is, the relationship of the Jews to the nations among whom they live, as well as to the state in general, together with the concurrent problem of Zionism as a question of the national character of Israel. This last area of debate, which has become pressing in recent years, is specifically modern, having been possible only since 1789. Since it leads into new areas, some quite beyond the scope of theology, it can be discussed, given the framework of this debate, only obliquely.

The questions are so closely related that Schmidt is forced to formulate them as one: "The only important question is whether nearly two thousand years ago the Jewish nation, the Jewish Church of that time, did not harden their hearts against the Messiah sent by God, thereupon, through the destruction of Jerusalem, losing the focus of their ramified

Diaspora, and thenceforth living in the Diaspora, in dispersion, without a spiritual center." (*Theologische Blätter,* September, 1933, p. 260) This sin (*sc.* the crucifixion of Jesus), he goes on, does not merely attach to the Jews, but, rather, discovers the sin of all mankind as represented in the Judaism of that period, that is, the sin of the entire world. As the chosen people, Israel had a special call to follow the Saviour; the special punishment for Israel was the destruction of Jerusalem, which left the Jewish Diaspora without a focus up to the present day. But Jerusalem will never again belong to the Jews. The efforts of Zionism are in vain, the more so since Zionism's idolization of the people as a natural nation is wholly contrary to Judaism. As a Christian and New Testament theologian, he, too, knows that the *true* Israel cannot understand its existence to be based on blood, but only on the call of God. Israel must view itself not as one nation among others, but as the especially distinguished *servant of God.* "Unlike the Jews, who reject the Messiah, Jesus of Nazareth, the Christians confess that the servant of God has appeared in personal form in *Jesus Christ.* It is only from this caesura that secular history can be understood as divine history, as *Heilsgeschichte.* The Church of Jesus Christ knows and proclaims this. It absolutely does not view Judaism as a danger in the sense of a national or political philosophy, because, as Israel, Judaism is necessarily on the road to the Church. The Jew who becomes a Christian leaves his unfulfilled Israel for the fulfilled Israel, the Church of Jesus Christ, the Israel after the spirit." (*Ibid.,* pp. 263 f.)

Buber's reply to the four disputed areas cannot likewise consist of declared dogmas; it is possible only as a confession based on the depth of his own faith, together with that share of the prophetic consciousness which Buber bears through the history of our time. The important thing is to bring two kinds of witness to confrontation: the Church's knowledge *about* Israel, and Israel's knowledge *of itself*. This is done first in discussing the question of Israel's election or rejection.

"The Church sees Israel as an entity *rejected* by God. This rejection follows necessarily from the Church's claim to be the true Israel: the members of Israel, accordingly, have surrendered their claim because they did not recognize Jesus as the Messiah. Christians believe they have received from God this 'being-Israel,' this office, the honor of Israel, its election; here is an assurance, grounded in faith, which is unassailable. We have no possibility of opposing anything to this, the Church's knowledge about Israel; anything so put forward would have only argumentative effectiveness. But we, as Israel, know Israel from within, in the darkness of knowledge from within, in the light of knowledge from within. We know Israel differently, we know (at this point I can no longer even say 'see,' for we know it from within, not even with the 'eye of the spirit,' but only as we live it) that we who have sinned a thousandfold against God, who have apostasized from God a thousandfold, who, throughout these centuries, have experienced God's providence over us —which it is too easy to call punishment; it is something greater than punishment—we know that we are, nevertheless, not rejected. We know that this is an event which does not take place within the limited perspective of this world, but in the reality of the space between God and us. We know that there, within that reality, we are not rejected by God, that in this discipline and punishment, God's hand holds us and does not let us go, holds us within this fire and does not let us fall." (*Die Stunde und die Erkenntnis,* pp. 149 f.)

This witness of Martin Buber to his faith coincides and intersects with the Jewish witness of life and suffering through the centuries. In his reply, directed to an audience made up of both Christians and Jews, Schmidt must answer as follows: "The depth of experience of a man living within the realm of Judaism by blood has been made clear to you, and also to me. It is more than a collection of miscellaneous events." (*Theologische Blätter,* page 272) Schmidt's further question, which he had previously asked in his introductory speech, was whether in Jesus the historically awaited Messiah of Judaism had arrived. He asked this, together with the related question of the absolute validity and exclusive nature of the Christian revelation (*extra ecclesia nulla salus*). Again Buber gives a *confessing* answer, based on his experience of Israel's knowledge of itself.

Karl Ludwig Schmidt has rightly placed the question of the Messiah, the Christological question, in the center of his observations.

If we want to express in a simple formula the difference between Jews and Christians, between Israel and the Church, we can say: the Church is grounded upon the belief that Christ has already come, redemption has been granted to men through God. We, as Israel, are unable to accept this belief.

The Church views our position either as unwillingness to believe, a hardness of heart in a very dubious sense, or as a constraint, a fundamental limitation of ability to perceive vis-à-vis reality, as the blinding of Israel which prevents it from seeing the light.

We, as Israel, understand our inability to accept this proclamation in another fashion. We understand the Christology of Christianity throughout as an important event which has taken place between the world above and the world below. We see Christianity as something the mystery of whose coming into the world we are unable to penetrate. But just as we know that there is air which we breathe into our lungs, we know also that there is a space in which we move; more deeply, more genuinely, we know that the history of the world has not yet been shattered to its very core, that the world is not yet redeemed. We feel the unredemption of the world.

The Church can or must understand this feeling as a conviction of *our* unredemption. But we understand it differently.

For us, the redemption of the world is indissolubly one with the perfecting of creation, with the establishment of a unity no longer limited in any respect, no longer suffering contradiction, realized in all the multiplicity of the world, one with the fulfilled kingdom of God. An anticipation of the completed redemption of the world to some partial extent, such as the redeemed state of the soul, we are unable to comprehend, no matter how redemption and the redemption process are proclaimed to us in our mortal hours.

We do not perceive any caesura in the course of history. We know of no mid-point in it, but only a goal, the goal of the way of God, who does not pause upon his way.[109]

We cannot define God under any aspect of his revelation. That statement from the burning bush: "I shall be present as he, as whom I shall be present" (i.e., as whom I shall be present at any given time), makes it impossible for us to take anything unique as the ultimate revelation of God. Not as though we could say anything of God's ability to reveal himself or not, as he may choose; I say only that we are unable to draw any absolute conclusions from all the revelations which we know. We do not say that God cannot reveal himself in this manner. We only say that we cannot ascribe finality to any one of his revelations, nor to any one the character of the Incarnation. Unconditionally, that futuristic word of the Lord points to the beyond at every moment of passing time; God transcends absolutely all of his manifestations. (*Ibid.,* pp. 153-155)[110]

This says something which is very important, formulating it almost more pointedly than did Rosenzweig: Christology (that is, the doctrine of the *reality* of the Christ-event) must be understood as an "important event which has taken place between the world above and the world below." This statement is spoken in the form "we as Israel." But with this statement by Buber, we must keep in mind the difference between "belief" and "acknowledgment" if we are to accept as admissable this recognition on the part of Judaism, the more so since Buber himself declares, a few sentences later: "We are not able to define God under any aspect of his revelation." And immediately thereafter: "We only say that we cannot ascribe finality to any one of his revelations, nor to any one the character of the Incarnation."

These restrictions on the part of Judaism, as they are expressed through Buber, facilitate greatly the dialogue with Christianity. But the question arises whether this relativization, perhaps pushed to an unnecessary degree by overemphasis, does not effect too great a separation from tradition. As a sensitive man of our day, Buber knows something enormously important, something that can be experienced only in life. It is not open to the man who, through the security of tradition, withdraws from real encounter with the questionable aspects of life, and thus also from the possibility of a crisis of the law. This law has its being not only in the stasis of tradition, but also, in accord with its imperative nature, in the future; it achieves its ultimate form neither in the Torah nor in that normative compendium of Jewish law the *Shulḥan 'Aruḳ;* rather, it can confront me, here and today, as something new, something actual, that is, an imperative reality. However, if the law is capable of being transcended, if God has not defined himself completely through his revelation, then the absolute character of divine revelation in history is made precarious. The Rabbis were never able to admit this, nor can a serious faith in the Christological dogma admit such a possiblity. Here is the thorn in the flesh, the final irresolution within history of the Judaeo-Christian antinomy. Israel and Christianity *must* assert the exclusive and ultimate nature of the revelation granted to each on the grounds of the truth of revelation itself; for, in fact, God cannot transcend his own word, which is absolute truth, if he does not wish to make a mockery of human belief. Thus revelation of God to the believer must be ultimate, incapable of being transcended. The only limitation which may be granted, the limitation in which we recognize the possibility for "progress" today, is that the Jewish revelation is ultimate and final only for its followers, that is, for the Jews; but the Jew of today, on the basis of his experience of historical reality, can admit that outside of Israel, other revelations may have taken place in the world which are without immediate meaning for Israel. As a universal religion with a missionary claim upon the Gentiles, that is, *all* non-Jewish mankind, by the very nature of the case, Christianity can never make this same admission; in such a case—quite apart from Israel—it would also have to recognize the divine origin of Islam. Buber's position in these discussions has yet to be finally clarified.[111] But the remaining vagueness is probably connected with the question he has not yet answered, concerning the historical uniqueness of the revelation-event and the concurrent *absolute validity* of the Mosaic Law as an unalterable covenant-charter for all Israel. Thus tradition has always understood it, in accordance with the words of Scripture (*sc.* in "faithfulness to the Torah"); modern non-Orthodox Judaism no longer acknowledges this, but up to now has not yet given a real answer to this burning question.

There remains Schmidt's question as to the possibility or impossibility of Zionism for the Jewish religion. Buber's response centers upon the dialectic affirmation of the state in general, and the acceptance of Israel as a nation by the Christian nations. Buber, too, is aware of the latent danger which Zionism represents as a possible secularization of Jewish historical truth. But nevertheless—his position today, with its inner dialectic, would probably have to be called that of a "marginal Zionist"—he recognizes the movement of Zionism as a justifiable corrective to the nineteenth century tendency to confessionalize Israel.

"Karl Ludwig Schmidt has asked me about Zionism. Certainly here the concept of nationhood has been emphasized and overemphasized. This has happened because, within an indissoluble union of national existence and faith, national existence was greatly neglected during the period of the emancipation. The attempt was made to allot Israel its place among the religions. In contrast to this, it had to be said by way of warning that Israel without its national existence has no reality. But today it is time once more to place the real Israel in the place of national and religious concepts—the unity and uniqueness of Israel." (*Ibid.*, p. 162)

"But within what secular categories does the true Israel fall? Can it be comprehended at all within these categories?

"I repeat: the fact that Israel exists is something unique, something which cannot be assigned a place within a system. This name, given by God to the patriarch, not by father and mother, characterizes the community as one which cannot be comprehended under the categories of ethnology and sociology. As soon as we make use of such a category, we do Israel an injustice. In the Bible it is declared what furnishes the basis of Israel's uniqueness. The Bible depicts the genesis of this community as identical, historically and factually, with the faith-experience and faith-action of a band of men in their decisive hour.

"This band of men experiences there something which encounters it as a believing band, a band united in faith, not as believing individuals but as a believing community; as such it hears and responds in faith. In this process of being addressed and making response, in that very hour it is con-

stituted that which we call a nation, an entity which thenceforth continues on in a closed circle of generations and births.
This sets off Israel for all time from nations and from religions." (*Ibid,* p. 156)

These statements are treated systematically on a biblical-
historical basis in Buber's unfinished magnum opus, *Das
Kommende.* In his reply, Schmidt agrees, to the extent that
he will not refuse Buber his agreement in the *essential* question, that "Israel cannot be apprehended as a mere religion
among other religions, as a mere nation among other nations." (*Ibid.,* p. 271) But if the history of Israel represents
the history of God's endeavors and labors on behalf of his
people, there belongs also among these the one described at
the beginning of the Epistle to the Hebrews: "In many and
various ways God spoke of old to our fathers by the prophets;
but in these last days he has spoken to us by a Son."

Schmidt continues further: "As I have already pointed out,
the New Testament emphasizes again and again that this
word, this action on the part of God, is not preliminary but
final, once and for all. In spite of this, we Christians, like the
Jews, look to the end. But we dare to do so only on the basis
of the fact that God in Jesus Christ has already caused the
end to be at hand. We now speak of the coming of Jesus
Christ at the end of time as his second coming, his return.
From this point of view, the association of the Christian with
the Jew is only preliminary. Were the Church more Christian than it is, the conflict with Judaism would be sharper
than it can be now. From the very beginning, this sharp
conflict has existed in the history of Christianity. We Christians must never tire of keeping this one conflict alive." (*Ibid.,*
pp. 272 f.)

Thus the witness of one faith stands opposed to that of the
other. But much has become clear. The evaluation of this

discussion reached by the missionary arm of Christianity was that it "will perhaps satisfy no one, because it puts each in the right, but also puts each in the wrong." (*Saat auf Hoffnung,* 1934, Heft 1) This may be true; but then, the intention is not to satisfy anyone, because the discussion has not yet been concluded. In the course of history, many more Judaeo-Christian discussions may have to be conducted—with the right and with the wrong inherent in each side.

In this religious debate at Stuttgart in 1933, the last word which Martin Buber had to speak is such an impressive witness to the genuine power of faith that we can think of no better plan than to reproduce it here word for word, without abbreviation, in order that it may bring to a close both this chapter and the history, up to the present day, of Judaeo-Christian arguments and debates. Here is expressed everything which can be expressed concerning the relationship between Israel and the Church, from the depth of the Jewish faith:

I live not far from the city of Worms, to which I am bound by a tradition of my forefathers; and, from time to time, I go there. When I go there, I go first to the cathedral. It is a visible harmony of members, a totality in which no part deviates from perfection. With consummate joy I walk about the cathedral, gazing at it. Then I go over to the Jewish cemetery. It consists of crooked, cracked, shapeless, random stones. I station myself there, gaze upward from the jumble of a cemetery to that glorious harmony, and it is as though I were looking up from Israel to the Church. Below, there's not a jot of form; there are only the stones and the ashes under the stones. The ashes are there, no matter how thinly they are scattered. There is the corporeality of men, which has turned to this. There it is. There it is for me. There it is for me, not as corporeality in the space of this planet, but as corporeality in my own memory, far into the depths of history, as far back as Sinai.

I have stood there, have been united with the ashes, and through them with the patriarchs. That is a memory of the transaction with God which is given to all Jews. From this the perfection of the Christian house of God cannot separate me, nothing can separate me from the sacred history of Israel.

I have stood there and have experienced everything myself; all this death has confronted me: all the ashes, all the ruin, all the wordless misery is mine; but the covenant has not been withdrawn from me. I lie on the ground, fallen like these stones. But it has not been withdrawn from me.

The cathedral is as it is. The cemetery is as it is. But nothing has been withdrawn from us.

Were the Church more Christian, were the Christians more sanctified, did they not have to remonstrate with themselves, then, says Karl Ludwig Schmidt, there would ensue a bitter argument between them and us.

Were Judaism once more to become Israel, were the sacred countenance to appear once more behind the mask, then I would reply, the separation would indeed continue unabated; but there would not be a more bitter argument between us and the Church, but, rather, something wholly different, which today is still ineffable.

I ask, finally, that you hear two statements which appear to contradict each other, but do not contradict each other.

The Talmud (Yebamot 47a) teaches: If in this age a proselyte comes in order to be received into Judaism, let him be told: "What have you seen among us, that you should want to be converted to it? Do you not know that the people of Israel in this age are tortured, battered, buffeted, driven about, that miseries have come upon them?" If he says, "I know, and I am not worthy," then let him at once be received.

It might appear that this is Jewish arrogance. It is not. It is nothing else than the proclamation that cannot be dismissed. The misery is real misery, and the disgrace is real disgrace. But in it there is a purpose of God, which promises to us that, as God has promised to us (Isa. 54:10), he will never let us fall from his hand.

The Midrash (Shemot Rabbah XIX, Sifra on Lev. 18:5) says: "The Holy One (blessed be he) declares no creature unworthy, but receives them all. Every moment the gates are open, and whoever seeks to gain entrance, gains entrance. And thus he says (Isa. 26:2): 'Open ye the gates, that the righteous nation [*goy ṣaddîk*] that keepeth faithfulness may enter in.' It is not said that priests shall come, that Levites shall come, that Israelites shall come; but it is said that a *goy ṣaddîk* shall come."

The first statement spoke concerning proselytes; the second does not; it speaks concerning the race of men. *The gates of God stand open to all. The Christian need not go through Judaism, the Jew need not go through Christianity, in order to come to God."* (*Die Stunde und die Erkenntnis*, pp. 165-167)

VIII

JEWISH REALITY
AND CHRISTIAN REALITY

1 REMARKS ON THE COMPARATIVE
PHENOMENOLOGY OF RELIGION

IN BROAD outline, we have followed the history of the
conflict between the Jewish and Christian faiths from the
period of the origin of Christianity through the Middle Ages,
the Enlightenment, and the nineteenth century, down to the
present. We have seen how the inner tendency of this conflict, the central questions which keep returning, progressed
from *argument* to *dialogue*. But we feel we should not close
without referring once more to our introductory remarks. On
the basis of our present knowledge, we may derive phenomenological results from the conclusions we have reached in
our study. For this, using our own language and point of
view, we shall attempt to outline the basic systematic problems which still confront further efforts.

Franz Rosenzweig's and Martin Buber's efforts to enter
into dialogue have presumably made amply clear that in the
present day, the Jewish postulates have undergone a fundamental change. There is a new state of affairs. In respect to
the reality of historical events, the Jewish side recognizes the

divine origin of Christianity and its revelation as the way of salvation for the Gentile world outside of Israel—although this act of recognition is and must be something quite different from an act of faith! This cannot be traditionally grounded in such a way that it could become valid *halakhah;* but it can become *minhâgh* (custom), which, in the realm of Judaism, often enjoys respect equal, if not superior, to halakhah. Since the time of Rosenzweig and Buber, this has to a large extent taken place. Indeed, in the future there will be no other way of speaking with the Church—whether the Church of Luther, or of Calvin, or of Rome—except upon the tacit assumption that "between the Church, which recognizes no limited sphere of authority, and Israel, which is conscious of its sphere of authority, there can be a genuine dialogue, in which the participants do not reach an agreement, but, rather, reach understanding, for the sake of the one true being which is behind the realities of faith." (Buber: *Die Stunde und die Erkenntnis,* p. 163)

If this is the outcome of the change to a new manner of thought, in the framework of which the first existential religious dialogues have already been conducted, it seems that something decisive has been gained and expressed. In the future, a Jew no longer needs, nor can afford, to greet the "results" of the study of the history of religions as an expression of lack of faith, and, depending on inclination and taste, either join Wellhausen and Harnack in worshiping Jesus as an archetypal man filled with the divine spirit, or Kalthoff in seeing in him the symbolic figure of a revolutionary social movement, or even Drews and Brandes in simply denying his existence and assuming that we have to do with nothing more than an Egyptian-Syrian nature myth. If modern, objective thought teaches anything, it is this: Historical effect can proceed only from historical reality; it is not to the point to seek to explain an event—especially a sacred event —from a point of view different from the one which explains itself.[112] This says nothing against the justification for historical study of religion; examining how a new reality grows in dialectical relationship with previous knowledge; acquiring synthetic form and final structure; or exploring the postulates and dispositions typical of an age, which form the starting point of a new doctrine, in order to bring their contribution before men. But one must remember that the nature of the Torah of Moses cannot be explained on the basis of apparently similar, or even identical, regulations in the Code of Hammurabi, or the ritual on the basis of parallel rites and customs of the Near East. Similarly, the ethics of Jesus' teaching is not explained by collecting the parallels from rabbinic sources. It should be noted in passing that the celebrated ethical "advance" of the Sermon on the Mount over Jewish morality—the favorite theme of the nineteenth century—provides the least suitable and most irrelevant measuring stick, or common denominator, for comparing Judaism with Christianity.

If one wishes to make this comparison—no idle task, if information is to be acquired about realities—the most important thing is not to compare the conceptions and doctrines of God, man, sin, grace, resurrection, and so forth. All these comparisons—similarities as well as differences—evolve from the mutual confrontation of the witness borne by Israel and Christianity as to their origin and their central mystery. This is not accomplished by extracting the older and newer layers from the present text of the Torah or the gospels in order to discover that stratum of tradition which reaches back the farthest, but is accomplished only by accepting the texts in their transmitted form, admittedly corrupt and often apparently contradictory. They are to be read for the purpose of discovering what they have to say; and what they say is to be believed in faith. Earlier generations of scholars, in their naïvete, often dealt more honestly with this question than do the critical scholars of our own day. On the other hand, thanks to their lack of preconceived notions, these latter have the great possibility of understanding everything that has been written, really on its own level, neither typologically, nor symbolically, nor by any other method which is not genuine. Today no one is required to abolish his critical faculties; this will not increase his faith. One is rather to be faithful *through* his critical and historical knowledge, without discarding it. Faithful, that is, to the belief that Torah and Gospel give an account of events of sacred history, in which the transcendent became real. Even today it can become real for each and every individual who has contact with the event described, or gains contact with it.

2 THE ESSENTIAL DIFFERENCE

If we are to state anything about the inmost nature of Judaism and the inmost nature of Christianity—in their essential difference—and pursue, in addition, the insights which the preceding arguments have brought to the attention of the reader, we must first establish, on a purely phenomenological basis, the following: It is not Church and Synagogue which confront each other, but, rather, Church and the people Israel. The *ecclesia* is a *spiritual* people called together *in* faith and *to* faith out of the peoples of the heathen world, summoned not by nature and descent, but by the Holy Spirit. In the Church of Jesus Christ, truly neither Jew nor Greek is valued according to origin, neither slave nor free according to social class; the *only* thing of value is the *new* creature, as it is writ-

ten, "Behold, all has been made new." The old Adam has
been expunged; the heathen who has turned Christian becomes, through the Holy Spirit, a *new* man, who comes to
the Father through Jesus Christ or through the Church, in
which Christ lives. In faith he participates in the coming of
Jesus Christ to the Father. That is the essence of the New
Covenant, nor can it be anything else if it is really to be a
covenant with mankind, a covenant for all mankind. In
Judaism, none of this is true. Israel does not need to be redeemed by an atoning sacrifice, because it has already been
elected by God. It has stood within the covenant ever since
the acceptance and accounting of Abraham's readiness to
sacrifice, so that even the apostate Jew—through *teshûbhâh*
(return)—need only return to the creature-situation of Abraham. In Isaac, all Jews, as "seed of Abraham" (the father of
a great nation), are become children of the promise, the content of which is the perpetual possibility of return—to Abraham's bosom. Return to the destiny of the original birth
does not demand, as in the case of the Christian, that one
be cleansed for a second birth, the rebirth in the Holy Spirit.
The people of Israel is spared the detour of faith, solely because Abraham was obedient to God. The election of the
seed of Abraham has already brought all paths to their goal:
whoever is born an Israelite is a member of the Covenant by
virtue of his birth. Thus the seed of Abraham became *zera*ʿ
ḳôdhesh, holy seed.

This ontological state (which is what all talk of election
ultimately means) is persistently misconstrued by all who
still see through the theological glasses of the nineteenth
century—as misconstrued as is the "law," which, as we have
shown, is meant neither to reconcile the Jew with God nor
to justify him before God; it was given, rather, as the con-
stitutive occasion of the Covenant. The Covenant effects sanc-

tification for the man who keeps it, as evidence of God's elective grace.

Here we shall once more discuss the essential difference *systematically*. As long as it is not fully understood, all dialogue between the two groups takes place in a vacuum. In this *new* view of the totality of religious phenomena resides the author's new theological insight and actual purpose, which he has sought to bring to light indirectly, in the *material* of historical presentation. Even from the point of view of religious phenomenology, *faith* is to be had by genuine *acknowledgment*. As long as this view is not really accepted by Christians, there can be scarcely anything more depressing for a Jew than what the Church says about Israel, today as always, without knowledge of Israel's understanding of itself. The Church even tries to persuade Israel of this view in its missionary efforts. It simply will not do that the Church should further refuse to ascribe to the Old Testament what by right belongs to it,[113] seeking in it always only the account of creation and its *own* prehistory. In this case, obviously it cannot understand concretely the legal reality of the Old Testament, which—concretely—is concerned with a *nation* in every phase of its organization. Without its covenant laws, Israel would not exist at all; therefore, the law certainly cannot be abrogated—at least not by an event within time which purports to be fulfillment. True fulfillment of the law would, in fact, be the end of all time, namely, the resurrection of all the dead who died under the law. And further: What is the Jew to make of the talk that the God of the Old Testament is primarily a God of justice, while the God of the New Testament is primarily a God of love, who, out of love for mankind, because the latter was unable to fulfill the law, himself became man in order through his *own* fulfillment of the law to fulfill it for all men? Statements of this kind have been made until they have become unbearable. The Jewish reply, if it is to be repeated here, can be only: Talk of this sort betrays a terrifying ignorance of what "covenant" and "law" are. The covenant was granted to a human nation by the free elective grace of God. Thenceforth, this nation, not by virtue of its corporeality, but by virtue of the divine will, became an immediate kingdom (*mamlâkhâh*), singled out (*kâdhôsh*) from among all nations (*see* M. Buber: *Königtum Gottes,* Berlin, 1936, p. 125). The law was given in order to lay upon the shoulders of each individual member of the covenant community the yoke of the kingdom of heaven, to set before his eyes the kingship of God—all the days of his life. He who fulfills his duty as a loyal subject and lives according to the Torah, shares in the foretaste of the future world by so living. Thus reads every Jewish explanation of the law which has been given in harmony with tradition.

But Paul understood the covenant and law contrary to their reality—that is, misunderstood them. Ever since, it has been the Christian notion of the law that it cannot be fulfilled by *man* (this is obvious to the Jew—it proves to man the law's divine nature), and therefore could no longer truly unite the *Jew* with God. This is the basic misunderstanding, for the covenant comes *before* the law, and the very intention of the Jew to fulfill it *is* this unity. Thus God was forced to create another bond of unity; out of his infinite love for mankind, he came down into flesh (an idea which, in our view, has real truth as far as the non-Israelite is concerned).[114] Such talk, directed at the Jews with the intention of proselytizing them, can be answered by the Jewish faith-consciousness only by the following statement, if we may formulate the matter quite sharply for the moment: God's love for man resides precisely in the fact that he does not become flesh, but *remains* God; that, as Lord over heaven and earth, he does not die on the cross as a forsaken man. If the love of God is to be brought into the discussion, it will not permit such a grotesque mockery of man as is effected by the abrogation of God's very transcendence. When Christians state that this —a stumbling block to the Jews—nevertheless really took place, we can either believe the datum they report, or not believe it. In any event, this falls outside of Israel, outside of what the Jew knows on the basis of the redemptive acts which are his inheritance and revelatory records of his covenant. What is basically new—and at the same time also the utmost limit of what is possible—is this: We believe it when they say it. Therein lies the Jewish acknowledgment we have alluded to, namely, to grant belief to the Christian witness that God has dealt with the world and a new revelation has taken place outside the covenant with Israel and the revelation to it. But this event, the conclusion of the New Covenant, can only be understood reflectively by the modern Jew. This New Covenant, of course, does not affect the covenant concluded with *him,* does not lie on the same plane as the law and biological election. Thus, also, it does not imply the election of another people; rather, it has taken place on a pneumatic plane above the level of all peoples—as the proclamation of salvation for *all* Gentile mankind, which, in spite of the Noachite laws, is not directly considered in the Torah. The recognition of other covenants outside of Israel (*sc.* the covenant of Christ, and, in principle, that of Mohammed) even fills a gap in Jewish knowledge, since, according to Jewish belief, not only Israel but all mankind belongs to God, and is called on the path to God. The truth of the covenant with Israel, which is properly called the Eternal Covenant, not the Old Covenant, is independent of human claims, and is not to be abrogated or revoked by God; for God is not a man, that He should lie; neither the son of man, that He should repent (Num. 23:19).

Here we must express the hope that, just as today we are prepared to acknowledge the witness of the Church to be true, as the truth which has been granted exclusively to the Church, so the Church may also acknowledge our awareness of God and his covenant with us as true, as the truth which has been granted exclusively to us, may find and rediscover the work of God not only in the Old Testament—that is, in the past tense—but also in the post-Biblical Synagogue, in Israel up to the present day. For in all seriousness, the blindness and hardness of heart of the Jews is not a "doctrine of substantial nature," but a human judgment, which can be amended. Then there can remain the essential content of the intention behind the dogmatic statement, namely, that the end of time will come only when "Old Covenant" and "New Covenant" have become One Covenant. Thus Buber, as a Jew, can formulate the newly won insight: "The mystery of another lies deep within him, and it cannot be observed from without. No man outside of Israel knows the mystery of Israel. And no man outside of Christianity knows the mystery of Christianity. But in their ignorance they can acknowledge each other in the mystery." (*Die Stunde und die Erkenntnis,* p. 155)

3 THE PRESENT HOUR

Up to now we have spoken of Israel and Christianity as two objective phenomena. But in the introductory remarks we defined an historical claim which will not have been honored unless we conclude our historical study by taking a glance at the present status of both religions. We shall do this by attempting to describe the adherents of both sides, Jews and Christians, in their contemporary situation, even though the formulation of these insights, on account of their proximity in time, can only be fragmentary. We may hint at the situation—the questions raised must remain questions —by stating the following:

Jews and Christians today are to a large extent in the same situation: that of *unbelief*. As is well known, a great caesura, a turning point in history, has occurred in the past one hundred and fifty years. The unbelief of previous ages always remained close to the periphery of positive belief; until Kierkegaard and Nietzsche, it possessed the dialectic tendency of turning into positive belief. In the most recent decades, a new situation has arisen: that of *unbelief*, which avoids dialogue —even polemic—with the witnesses and bearers of belief. Its attitude toward the saving events witnessed to by the centuries is not one of doubt and uncertainty, but of unbelief and lack of interest. Today the pagan baptized in the Church does not become a Christian by virtue of his baptism alone, since baptism no longer integrates him *realiter* into a living Christian society. On the other side, what meaning attaches to birth within the covenant of Abraham when the person so born no longer feels that he stands within the context of the covenant of election, but, rather, *de facto* in other contexts, possibly even contradictory to that of his calling. The truth possessed by Israel and the truth possessed by the Church do not thereby become less true; as such, they cannot be assailed by historical processes. But for about one hundred and fifty years, both have been losing effectiveness and reality within the world to an increasing degree. This is a portentous happening; it has not gone unnoticed, but today is becoming ever more plain and more threatening. It stands in need of responsible discussion in other contexts.[115] Here our task is only to state the fact. We cannot avoid the observation that the religious disputations of the Middle Ages, even though not real dialogues, at least held the attention of the world. Where has the world gone—or, rather, what else has attracted its attention? The answer is: post-Christian and unJewish events. It makes no sense to shut our eyes to the post-Christian condition of the world today, continuing credulously to believe that the modern forces of science and the industrial world, of collectives and nationalisms, can still be christianized by the Church. This age is no longer an age of the Judaeo-Christian faith; by objective criteria, it is already something quite different. The best course for men of the Church and the Synagogue is probably to remain without illusions; and where there is faith, there are no more illusions. Possibly this age, too, will advance to renewed faith. But in all probability this will not be a faith to which Church or Synagogue can lay claim. The human understanding of self and the world has been so transformed, and continues so to be transformed, that the individual Christian and the individual Jew—to say nothing of Church and Synagogue— can no longer affect the course of history, or alter it through confession of faith. But verily he will not despair on this account: he will leave the matter to him who is and remains the Lord of history. The dialogue which Christian and Jew have conducted with each other and continue to conduct will remain in the future. But the dialogue has lost its effect upon the world, and will continue to lose its effect, for today Israel and Christianity live upon islands and must carry on their dialogue from one island to the other. Between them both, and around them, swirls the flood of history, seeking to overwhelm even these islands.

Franz Rosenzweig clearly saw this development coming. In one of the last statements he made during his life, he writes that Synagogue and Church, in the future, probably will no longer be able to affect the course of humanity;

dogma and law will continue to exist only for small nuclear groups (*Jüdische Enzyklopädie,* IV, 751)—as the prophetic word of the "remnant" of Israel and the "remnant" of the nations foretold. This development may even have its good side for Judaeo-Christian dialogue. For ultimately, the "historical facts" must dissolve obstructions which have so long stood between them, in the form of Christian power and Jewish impotence. Today the Church must experience in its body what for two thousand years the Jews have called *gâlûth,* ever since they lost their ancestral homeland, only to be confronted time after time with the loss of their new homes among the Gentiles. Today the Church, too, is experiencing the bitterness of being "only" a wanderer on the face of the earth. It is experiencing its Babylonian captivity —quite differently, much more concretely, than the Reformers ever thought.

But even this event in divine—or perhaps demonic—history, which unauthorizes all religious authority and confutes all religious confidence, may have its meaning for the salvation of the world. Today a reality is becoming clearer, a reality which no longer can be preached away: we can see in all seriousness the meaning and consequences of a duty to stand *against* the world. The number of temptations to conclude a compromise has become as great as the number of false paths. But perhaps Israel and the Church have never been nearer to the reality of their purpose than they are today, when the "remnant of Israel" is hidden among a swarm of "non-Aryans" (i.e., descendants from a common center of origin, which no longer has religious significance for the individual will and consciousness), and the organized Church is so far from the *Ecclesia invisibilis.* We cannot discuss here the possible meaning and consequences within the world and within sacred history of this disassociation, since this question lies at the very boundary of our subject of inquiry. But on the other hand it may be expected, in return, that the life of faith which endures among the remnant will increase in intensity, even though these discussions about God and his revelation, man and his salvation, take place far removed from the realm of contemporary history, and are no longer in the public eye. All this makes no difference to faith, for its inner vitality does not depend on this, and its power of witness remains undiminished, even if it no longer convinces pagans. The actual history of faith is internal. It has hidden depths into which only the eye of God can see. Out of all the changes that may be taking place there, the human eye can perceive this: Today, quite different sides of biblical reality are entering into the realm of history. Almost forgotten words of the ancient Bible are once more audible to us, words which the previous century no longer heard, or, if they did, understood contrary to their meaning. On the Christian side, the apocalyptic-eschatological theme seems today to be gaining the same actuality which biblical messianism is receiving on the Jewish side. If all the signs do not deceive, since the time of Buber and Rosenzweig, many segments of Israel no longer understand and experience law and covenant on an individual basis, but on an historical basis. This means that today an insight is possible which was no longer available to the orthodoxy of yesterday, because it had done away with everything dynamic for the sake of an eternal stasis, thus perversely allowing covenant and law to fall outside the framework of history. This insight is that, according to the nature of its formation, the covenant is eschatological, and the law, futuristic. Thus both—now at this point it may finally be said—yet stand in need of fulfillment, especially today, when the majority of Jews in Western Europe have fallen away from the traditional way of life, and, at best, live according to the law only by intention.

But deep inside, there is no other need than that of the Church of Christ itself, which likewise awaits ultimate fulfillment—namely, the return of its Lord. Having given itself to the world for centuries, today the Church discovers anew that it is lost in the world, especially today, when the Christian way of life is falling increasingly into desuetude, and the major portion of Christians baptized in the Church can scarcely be distinguished from non-Christians in the conduct of their lives.

The difference between the ways through history, as our eye sees it, has been brought to light; but it is not a difference of beginning, nor of the final hour. The messianism of Israel is directed toward that which is to come; the eschatology of the universal Gentile Church toward the return of Him who has come. Both are united by one common expectation, that the truth, which we do not know, which we can only guess, is *yet to come,* in that hour when the beginning is swallowed up in the end. At this point *all* Judaeo-Christian dialogue ends in the ancient petition of the Pater Noster: "Thy kingdom come to us," just as the New Testament, conscious of its own unfulfillment, with its concluding words, utters the prayer, "Amen. Come, Lord Jesus!"[116] And the Ḳaddish prayer of the Jew concludes with the same petition for fulfillment, of which no one knows whether it may come tomorrow, for the messianic kingdom which, in spite of all deceptions and disappointments, always is awaited in the day to come with the same fervor—morning, afternoon, and evening of every day of this aeon: "May he bring his kingdom to dominion within your lifetime and within your days and within the lifetime of the whole house of Israel—shortly, within a brief time."

NOTES

1   For more exact orientation in this period, see the still unsurpassed work of Leopold Lucas: *Zur Geschichte der Juden im vierten Jahrhundert* (Berlin, 1910). It contains especially valuable material for Jewish history from the writings of the Church Fathers. Cf. now also B. Blumenkranz: *Die Judenpredigt Augustins, ein Beitrag zur Geschichte der jüdisch-christlichen Beziehungen in den ersten Jahrhunderten* (Basel, 1946); and M. Simon: *Verus Israel, Étude sur les relations entre Chrétiens et Juifs dans l'Empire Romain* (135-425) (Paris, 1948); and most recently, H. J. Schoeps: *Paulus, die Theologie des Apostels im Lichte der jüdischen Religionsgeschichte* (Tübingen, 1959), chap. VI.

2   *Das Judentum und seine Umwelt* (Berlin, 1927). For the pre-Christian development of the term *"gêr"* from "stranger in the land" to "proselyte," cf. the monograph of A. Bertholet: *Die Stellung der Israeliten und der Juden zu den Fremden* (Freiburg, 1896); also S. Bialoblocki: *Die Beziehungen des Judentums zu Proselyten und Proselytismus* (Berlin, 1930).

3   Probably the oldest passage in rabbinic literature in which *yir'ê shâmayim* means "devout Gentiles" is in Mekilta on Exodus 22:20 (Winter-Wünsche translation, pp. 305 f.).

4   The best orientation to the halakhic side of this question is given by D. Hoffmann: *Der Schulchan 'Aruch und die Rabbinen über das Verhältnis der Juden zu Andersgläubigen* (Berlin, 1885), pp. 145 ff.; in addition, A.

Liebermann: *Zur jüdischen Moral* (Berlin, 1920), pp. 70 ff.; J. S. Bloch: *Israel und die Völker nach jüdischer Lehre* (Berlin-Vienna, 1932). There is also important material in the thick volume of the Italian cabalist Elie Benamozegh: *Israel et l'humanité* (Paris, 1914).

5   A comprehensive list of passages is given by L. Zunz: *Zur Geschichte und Literatur* (Berlin, 1919, second edition), pp. 371-389.

6   Numerous parallels can be cited for this view, which was typical of the current medieval conception. According to Isaac Abrabanel (commentary on Isaiah, 34:5), who may be cited at this point, the same relationship obtains between Israel and Christianity as between Jacob and Esau. According to the flesh and according to the spirit, they both have one father; they affirm the creation of the world and condemn idolatry; they recognize the law of Moses as divine, and worship God, even though in a manner which differs in perfection and appropriateness. But, in addition, Esau's hate toward Jacob also animates the Christian in his attitude toward the Israelite, making the latter's exile bitter.

7   One look inside the Misheh Torah, the Shulḥan 'Aruch, or any other halakhic work, suffices to determine the past and present shape of the Jewish moral teaching concerning behavior of the Jews toward their non-Jewish environment. We shall give here, as an example, one passage from the *Sepher Ḥasidim* (Book of the Devout) of R. Judah ha-Ḥasid, a book of moral instruction composed in Germany (Regensburg) at the end of the twelfth century and widely circulated among the Jewish population: "Deceive no one through any action, not even a Gentile. No one should be done injury, not even a member of another faith. In business transactions with Gentiles, deal with the same honesty as with Jews. When possible, point out to the Gentile his errors," etc. (pp. 7, 51, 74, 311, etc., frequently repeated).

8   Intended are the oxen which, at the Feast of Tabernacles, the High Priest formerly sacrificed in the temple at Jerusalem on behalf of the seventy nations of mankind (according to the list of Genesis 10) for their absolution.

9   Further material in Laible-Dalman: *Die talmudischen Texte über Jesus*

(Leipzig, 1900); and H. Strack: *Jesus, die Haeretiker und die Christen* (Leipzig, 1910). For a critical evaluation of sources from the Jewish point of view, cf. S. Krauss: *Das Leben Jesu nach jüdischen Quellen* (Berlin, 1902); and especially Joseph Klausner: *Jesus von Nazareth* (Berlin, 1930); and S. Zeitlin: "Jesus in the early tannaitic literature," *Abhandlg. z. Erinnerung an H. P. Chajes* (Vienna, 1933).

10 Anyone who desires to quote texts from the Midrash, Mishnah, and Talmud, using them to prove anything, almost invariably needs, first of all, an exact interpretation of the text, based on the period of origin of each passage quoted, its historical background, condition, and counterparts, the antiquity of the tradition in question, as well as its origins, etc. In this process, a large part is played by the corpus of traditional hermeneutics, which has not yet been systematically treated. This, starting from specific rules of exegesis, studies the particular use of scriptural quotation in Mishnah and Gemara, and on this basis seeks to understand the nature and intellectual structure of haggadic exegesis. In this study, critical evaluation of the sources has generally been avoided in particular cases; on the one hand, it would have destroyed the clear outline of our presentation; on the other, this work is not intended to be merely a scholarly study, which seldom has any further function—though this can be very important—than "enriching the field of study." The reader may be assured that every effort has been made not to quote arbitrarily, but that in the selection of texts which are intended to indicate and clarify the opinions and convictions representative of Jewish historical consciousness, great care has been taken.

11 A valuable beginning (unfortunately not continued) for the first three centuries after Christ was made by J. Bergmann: *Jüdische Apologetik im neutestamentlichen Zeitalter* (Berlin, 1908). Besides the books and articles of M. Güdemann, M. Friedländer, and A. Marmorstein, there is a commendable small work by J. Ziegler: *Der Kampf zwischen Judentum und Christentum in den ersten drei nachchristlichen Jahrhunderten* (Berlin, 1907), which only occasionally damages excellent statements of the problems through moralizing conceptions in the theological style of the turn of the century. A history of the Christian polemic *Adversus Judaeos* can now be found in the work of A. Lukyn Williams: *Adversus Judaeos, A Bird's-Eye View of Christian Apologiae Until the Renaissance* (Cambridge, 1935). Further, cf. James G. Parkes: *The Conflict of the Church and the Syna-*

gogue (London, 1934). Further literature, since the Second World War, is collected in the bibliography at the end of the book.

12 The replies are usually indirect, clothed in metaphorical language;· they often contain oblique references which can hardly be caught, the relevance of which we occasionally no longer recognize or can only guess at more or less vaguely. Information about direct debates with *mínîm*, who clearly must have been Christians, is preserved in writing from the Amora living in Lydda, R. Joshua ben Levi (e.g., Ber. 7a; Shemot rabbah 29, 4; and *passim*), as well as the heads of the academy in Caesarea, which had already been founded under the Tanna Bar Kappara, one of whose discussions is reproduced in I. J. Sabb. 6a. This school received the name of "the school of intellectual struggle with Christianity" (Baeck, in MGWJ, 1925, p. 264). Here the principal disputants were the son of the founder, R. Eliezer ha-Kappar (Yalkut Shimeoni 765, 66), the redactor of the Tossefta, R. Hoshaiah (Ber. Rabbah I, 1; and *passim*), and R. Abbahu (T. J. Ta'anit 65b; Shemot Rabbah 29, 5). These were Palestinian Amoraim of the second and third generation in the third century, living closest to the locale of the events. An excellent debater in Antioch was R. Simlai (T. J. Ber. IX, 1; Ber. Rabbah IX), as well as the Babylonian R. Idit (Sanh. 38b; Yalkut Shemot 359), both of whom taught in the third century. This by no means exhausts the list of Jewish disputants.

13 For example, cf. W. Vischer: *Das Christuszeugnis des A.T.,* vol. I (Zürich, 1946), or the work of one of Barth's pupils, Hans Hellbard: *Der verheissene König Israels (Das Christuszeugnis des Hosea)* (Munich, 1935).

14. Cf. also Leo Baeck: *Das Evangelium als Urkunde der jüdischen Glaubensgeschichte,* in "Paul, die Pharisäer und das Neue Testament" (Frankfurt, 1961).

15 This could also be reflected by the passage from the Midrash, Samuel V:4, which, interpreting the Jewish confession of faith, "Hear, O Israel" (Deut. 6:4), clearly has the Christological doctrine in mind: "If you turn the *daleth* [the third Hebrew letter] of the word *'ehâdh* (one) into a *resh,* [which in form is similar to a *daleth*] you destroy the world." This probably explains the fact that both in orthodox mahsorim and already in the

masoretic text of the Bible, the *daleth* is printed in boldface, twice its normal size, so that any misreading (*'aḥer* means "other" and was used as a locution for extreme apostates and for Jesus!) is excluded.

16 Similarly, Justin Martyr's *Dialogus cum Tryphone Judaeo*—a work of patristic literature—preserves views on the messiahship and soteriology of Jesus, asserted by the Christians, which were typical for Hellenistic Judaism. In chap. 38, we read, "You, O man, are pronouncing great blasphemies when you state that the crucified one was with Moses and with Aaron, spoke with him out of the pillar of cloud, then became man and, after death on the cross, ascended into heaven, that he will come again and that he must be worshiped." And chap. 48: "You are representing a paradoxical, thoroughly unprovable doctrine. For, if you say that this Christ was at all times God, then was born as man and was yet not a man born of human flesh, that is not only absurd, but stupid."

17 Jewish sources have nothing to say of any *crucifixion* of Jesus; nor can they, because crucifixion was never a Jewish method of execution. Furthermore, it is today historically clear (cf. H. Lietzmann: *Der Prozess Jesu,* Sonderberichte der Preussischen Akademie d. Wiss., phil.-hist. Klasse [Berlin, 1931]) that the Palestinian Jews about the year 30 had the right of accusation in the judicial process, but were no longer authorized to carry out executions. There is much instructive material on the trial of Jesus from the political point of view and from the point of view of the religious law in E. Stauffer: *Jesus, Gestalt und Geschichte,* Dalp-Taschenbücher, vol. 332 (Bern, 1957), pp. 92 ff.

18 Cf. now *Näheres in Agadisches zur Auserwählung Israels,* Conj. Neotest. VI (Uppsala, 1942), reprinted in my *Aus frühchristlicher Zeit* (Tübingen, 1950).

19 Cf. Rashi's explanation of the passage, which quotes the Midrash in Hullin 89a: "The Holy One, blessed be he, said to Israel: I have desire unto you, for even if I let greatness flourish upon you, yet you humble yourselves before me. I gave Abraham greatness, and he said to me: I "am but dust and ashes." (Gen. 18:27) Moses and Aaron said: ". . . what are we?" (Exod. 16:8) And David said: "But I am a worm, and no man." (Ps. 22:6) But not so are the nations of the world.

20 Once more, prophetic proof, especially in patristic literature, plays a great role in exegesis. Particularly the "Shiloh" passage, Genesis 49:10, has achieved a certain fame in this regard: "The sceptre shall not depart from Judah, nor the ruler's staff from between his feet, as long as men come to Shiloh; and unto him shall the obedience of the peoples be." Christian exegetes preferred to interpret this extremely obscure passage as a prophecy of Jesus—the expectation of the nations—and as a calling of the heathen, while Jewish commentators refer it to various historical persons or interpret it as referring to the future. (Cf. A. Posnanski's history of the exegesis of this verse: *Schiloh, ein Beitrag zur Geschichte der Messiaslehre* [Leipzig, 1904]).

21 The doctrine of the rejection of Israel, as J. Bergmann has shown (*op. cit.* p. 145), has also penetrated into Islam, which, of course, also designates the Christians as heretics. In the "Pater Noster" of Islam, it says: "Lead us in the right path, the path of those upon whom thou has bestowed mercy, who do not stand under wrath (*sc.* Jews) and who do not go astray (*sc.* Christians)."

22 The question whether rabbinic interpretation always reproduces the *peshât* (literal meaning) of the Bible passages must, of course, receive a negative answer. This can hardly be denied, even by an orthodox believer in the sacred character of the oral tradition and also the inspiration of the talmudic rabbis. The problems of Jewish hermeneutics cannot be discussed here.

23 Leo Baeck ("Zwei Beispiele midraschischer Predigt," MGWJ, 1925, pp. 266 ff.) was surely correct to understand this homily of Simon ben Yohai as an indirect answer to Christology. He understands similarly the great homily of R. Judah ben Simon on the locus of the *shekinah*, with which the Pesiktah of Rab Kahanah begins, and to which there are many parallels. In these, special emphasis is laid upon the fact that since the time of Abraham, the *shekinah* has been brought down from one heaven to the next through the righteous, finally attaining its place in the tabernacle and continuing in the shrines of Israel, its academies, and synagogues. Baeck concludes that it is meant to imply the following proposition: "The *shekinah* did not descend in Christ, nor does it have its lasting abode in the Church. The time of fulfillment did not come only with Christ, but began at Sinai—this moment when God once again has his domain upon earth."

24 See T. J. Berakot 13b: "Men commonly acknowledge only rich relatives, denying the poor; but even in its deepest humiliation God calls Israel brother and friend."

25 This idea has, in fact, been expressed several times: for example, by R. Hoshaiah (Palestine, c. 200) in Pesaḥim 87b: "The Holy One, blessed be his name, showed mercy to Israel by dispersing it among all the nations." In support of this view, it is stated that—even though persecution break out in one location within the exile—on account of its dispersion, Israel can be mutilated, but never destroyed. The material of historical experience gives adequate backing to this conviction!

26 The parallel statement by R. Eleazer ha-Ḳappar (Tanna of the second generation) is ambiguous. Cf. the doubts of H. Wenkschkewitz, *Angelos* IV (Leipzig, 1932), p. 91, covering Goldschmidt's translation of the passage.

27 Edom (synonomous with "kingdom of Esau") is already customary in the more recent portions of haggadah as a designation for Rome and the Christian Church. One of the first identifications with the biblical Edomites is probably the use of the term "kingdom of Esau" for Rome in IV Ezra 6:9, dating from about A.D. 100 (cf. also Gunkel's explanation of the passage). This objective basis for this use of the name is given by a legend reported in the second chapter of *Yosippon,* a medieval chronicle: Sefo (= Janus), a grandson of the biblical Esau—named Edom—came into the land of the Ḥittim (Romans) and ruled over it. (Cf. also J. Abrabanel: "Commentary on Isaiah," chapter 34, and David Ḳimḥi's interpretation of Joel 3:19.) Through the establishment of the episcopate of the Church in Rome, the Christians may be considered Edomites (according to the cabalists, the soul of Esau was even passed on to Jesus). All passages referring to these namesakes could henceforth be read eschatologically and interpreted as referring to the Christians. Medieval literature makes copious use of this association by symbolizing Edom as boundless drive for power and the principle of brute force. "Red (a pun: Edom-Adom) is man and land, red the food, the warrior, and his costume" (Ber. Rabbah 63, 12).

28 I have discussed this thoroughly in my work *Die Tempelzerstörung des Jahres 70 in der jüdischen Religionsgeschichte,* Coniectanea Neotesta-

mentica VI (Uppsala, 1942), reprinted in my collection of articles, *Aus frühchristlicher Zeit* (Tübingen, 1950).

29 The Roman *gâlûth* is usually interpreted as the fourth beast of the vision in Daniel 7:11. Other specific explanations are given, based on the biblical account of Jacob and Esau (Israel and Rome), which trace the punishment of the nation back to Jacob's sin against Esau and the lack of firmness of the patriarch's faith. Thus in his dream of the ladder, Jacob foresaw the four exiles, and, when he saw that of Edom, he feared that this kingdom would rule until the end of the world; but God comforts him with the verse from Jeremiah (30:10), "Fear thou not, O Jacob my servant," referring also to Obadiah 1:1-3, which states that Edom shall be cast down from on high. Nevertheless, Jacob does not trust the word of God, and so God decrees Israel's long-enduring subservience to the kingdoms. This, however, is not to last for eternity, "for"—so ends God's message—"I punish you through suffering in this world, in order to free you from your sins for the world to come" (following Gen. Rabbah 29 and the Pesiḳath of R. Kahana, Pisḳa 23).

Later on, Israel's subjection in the Edomitic *gâlûth* furnished mysticism with an occasion for deep speculations, which the cabalists read out of the biblical account of Jacob and Esau. Thus the Yalḳut Ḥadash (1648) gives the following reasons: (1) Because Jacob, who was holy, made himself unholy before Esau and did not obey the commandment of Genesis 25:23 (the elder shall serve the younger). In return, God swore that Edom should reign over Israel in this world, but Israel would have dominion in the world to come. (2) On account of Joseph's enslavement, and the fact that he was twelve years in prison, the punishment of life in the Edomitic misery has come upon the twelve tribes. (3) The *gâlûth* and all the plagues come on account of Esau's tears. This last clearly refers to an oral tradition, such as is preserved in Midrash Tehillim 80, 8: "Lord of the universe! For Esau's three tears hast thou allotted to him dominion over the world and given him prosperity; how much more shouldest thou look upon the humiliation of thy children and the endless tears of Israel."

30 The typical historical development in the direction of a spiritualizing doctrine of substitution following the destruction of the temple and the cessation of the sacrificial cult is well known and can be mentioned only in passing. The presentation of sacrifice in the temple is replaced primarily by three equivalents: study of the Torah, prayer, and good works. We

shall give one reference for each of these substitutes. For the study of the Torah: R. Aḥa said in the name of R. Ḥanina ben Papa (Amora of the third generation): "Formerly we presented sacrifices and were occupied with that; now that the sacrifices are no more, with what shall we occupy ourselves? To this God answers: 'Since you occupy yourselves with this, it is in my eyes as though you had presented the sacrifices.'" (Wayyiḳra Rabbah 8) For prayer: R. Joshua ben Levi (Amora of the first generation) said: "The prayers were so ordered as to correspond to the daily sacrifices, i.e., the recitation of the tefillah has taken the place of the daily sacrifice of Israel." (Berakot 26b) For good works: R. Joḥanan ben Zakkai, the greatest teacher at the time of the destruction of the temple, came one time with his pupil Rabbi Joshua to the site of the destruction, which previously had effected propitiation for the sins of Israel. When he saw his pupil crying to look upon this, he spoke to him: "My son, let it not displease you! We have a propitiation which is like to that. Which is that? It is demonstrations of love." (Abot of Rabbi Nathan IV) In the next generations, fasting, penance, humility, and the chastisements of fate are viewed as substitutions, and on this basis are taken into the maḥsorim. Concerning the sacrificial character of suffering, R. Nehemiah (Tanna of the third generation) says: "Beloved are sufferings, for just as sacrifices gain God's good will, so today suffering gains God's good will." (Mekiltah on Exod. 20:23) Cf. also the thorough presentation of these associations in Wenschkewitz, *op. cit.*, pp. 94 ff. The primary and most evident means of propitiation is seen by many as the punishment of exile itself, as Rabbi Joḥanan states: *"Gâlûth* is propitiation for everything." (Sanh. 37b)

31 Rabbi Judah said: "In the day when the Son of David comes, the synagogues will become brothels. The wisdom of the scribes will stink of decay. Those who are afraid of sin will be despised. The faces of the men of this age will be as those of dogs and truth will be wanting, as it is written in Isaiah: 'Truth is lacking, and he that departeth from evil maketh himself a prey.'" (59:15) R. Nehemiah: "In the age in which the Son of David comes, impudence will be great, and the unrighteous man will receive the most honor. The vine will bear fruit, and yet wine will be expensive." R. Isaac: "The Son of David will come only when the authorities have lapsed into heresy." An anonymous interpretation: The Son of David will not come until the Israelites have despaired of redemption.

Two conversations have been preserved between R. Eliezer ben Hyrkanos and R. Joshua ben Ḥananiah, and between Rab and Samuel, on the question whether penance and good deeds have any influence on the coming of redemption or whether redemption is the exclusive and unconditional realization of the grace of God. In both cases the decision remains open, but seems to tend more in the latter direction. According to R. Eliezer, redemption presupposes repentance. According to R. Joshua, it is independent of any work of man. Both provide scriptural quotations in support of their statements, until R. Eliezer can make no reply to Daniel 12:7: "a time, times, and a half; and when they have made an end of breaking in pieces the power of the holy people, all these things shall be finished." (T. J. Taan. 63d) The other dialogue consists of two statements only. Rab said: All calculations of the coming of redemption are already expired (without result). The matter depends now only upon penance and good deeds. But R. Samuel answered him: It suffices that he who bears suffering remains in his suffering (Sanh. 97b). That is: redemption is already resolved and will even come without penance and good deeds!

32 On this section, cf. now my book *Paulus, die Theologie des Apostels im Lichte der jüdischen Religionsgeschichte* (Tübingen, 1959).

33 A. Marmorstein, one of the outstanding scholars in the area of first-century Judaism, similarly gives his impression of the way in which the Tannaim interpreted the law in his work, *Judaism and Christianity in the Middle of the Third Century:* "The law was the most eloquent sign of God's love for his people Israel. The Tannaitic Haggadah preserves a number of sayings intended to bring home this truth. The Mizwot have no other function to man from God, than to increase man's holiness." *Studies in Jewish Theology* (London, 1950), p. 209.

34 In order to ascertain the true convictions of the Jewish faith throughout the centuries, even the Christian will still have to turn to the Jewish prayers. As typical of countless other portions, we cite here a section from the daily morning prayer, *"Ribbon ḳol ha-ʿolamim"* (written by R. Joḥanan): "Lord of all worlds! Not trusting in our own merit do we pray before thee, but trusting in thy great mercy. What are we, what is our life, what our love, what our devotion, what our help, what our strength, what our might, what should we say of thee, Lord, our God and God of our fathers? Heroes are as nothing before thee, and men of great name as though they had never been, and wise men as though without knowledge,

prudent men as though without prudence. For the number of their deeds is vain and the days of their life are nothing before thee." Further examples are given in my article, "Zur Theologie des jüdischen Gebetbuchs" (*Judaica,* Basel, 1948, vol. 2).

35 It cannot be overlooked that Paul carefully anticipated the possibility of this answer with the immediate statement that here he means "the word of faith which we preach" (Rom. 10:8), and not the bogey of "righteousness which comes through the law," of which Moses (supposedly!) wrote. Precisely on the basis of such a passage, the unprejudiced reader should be able to understand the rabbinic accusation of falsifying the scriptures directed against the Christians, even though here, as elsewhere, Paul desires to be understood typologically.

36 This must be admitted by even such a radical critic as Detlef Nielsen: *Der dreieinige Gott in religionsgechichtlicher Beleuchtung* (Copenhagen, 1922). In agreement with Baudissin, Jeremias, Gressmann, *et al.*, he summarizes his studies on page 388: "Pauline and Johannine theology, which late became determinative for the Christian Church, developed in Syria under the influence of non-Jewish Hellenistic culture. *Within Palestine, Jesus was never considered as God or Son of God.* In order to understand the origin of the divine, mythological Jesus, we must look at non-Jewish Semitic religion under the influence of Hellenism."

37 The decision of Paul and Barnabas reported in Acts 13:46 is based, likewise, on a divine command, which can be derived without difficulty from Isaiah 49:6.

38 Historical "Jewish Christianity" was only an episode in the history of the Church. Later baptisms of Jews were invariably individual occurrences, never signifying a radical change. On Jewish Christianity (or Ebionism) in the ancient Church and its fate, cf. H. J. Schoeps: *Theologie und Geschichte des Judenchristentums* (Tübingen, 1949).

39 G. Kittel *et al.* are of the opinion that this mishna, proposed by R. Eliezer of Modeim, refers immediately to the Apostle Paul. Proof of this can hardly be given; it is, nevertheless, certain that Paul's doctrines are *included* in this condemnation.

40   Reference should here be made to an interesting passage from Midr. Song of Songs 1:14 (similarly also Ber. Rabbah 47), where Rabbi Levi (*c.* 300), in the name of Rabbi Ḥama (*c.* 260) has Abraham express doubts before God on account of the covenant with Noah and any future covenants. God banishes this fear by referring to his promise that from Abraham's flesh there shall spring righteous men, who shall be present in every age, and atone for the sins of the children of Abraham. The belief in vicarious atonement, which can be heard here, is not uncommon in rabbinic literature. Systematic Jewish theology, on its usual basis, would have to derive it from the doctrinal concept of the *ṣekhûth 'âbhôth* (merit of the fathers). Cf. in this regard, A. Marmorstein: *The Doctrine of Merits in the Old Rabbinical Literature* (London, 1920).

41   Paul (Rom. 4:13 ff.; and *passim*) lays great emphasis on the doctrine that the promise of world inheritance made to Abraham and his seed is not mediated through the law, but stems from the righteousness of faith. This is good rabbinic teaching, and is represented in the Mekiltah in the name of the old head of the Sanhedrin, R. Shemiah (first century after Christ)—also anonymously in Shemot Rabbah 23.

42   The best orientation is given by Julius Guttmann: *Die Philosophie des Judentums* (Munich, 1935; Eng. trans., New York, 1963).

43   We may mention the most important representatives of this particular literary genre of the Middle Ages: Jacob ben Reuben: Milḥamot Adonai (1170); Joseph Ḳimḥi: *Sefet ha-Berit* (1170); Isaac Shaprut: *'Eben Boḥan* (1380); Profiat Duran: *'Al tehi ḳà-Aboteḳa* (1396) and *Kelimmat ha-Goyim* (1397); Ḥasdai Crescas: *Biṭṭul 'Iḳḳere ha-Noṣrim* (1410); Isaac Pulgar: *'Ezer ha-Da'at* (1420); Yomtob Lipmann Mülhausen: *Niṣṣahon* (1420); Isaac ben Abraham Troki: *Ḥizzuḳ 'Emunah* (1593); Leon de Modena: *Magen wa Ḥereb* (1630); Manasseh ben Israel: *Vindiciae Judaeorum* (1656). The most recent treatment of the dialogue-literature found in the Latin Church Fathers is B. Blumenkranz: "Die jüdischen Beweisgründe im Religionsgespräch mit den Christen in den christlichlateinischen Sonderschriften des 5.-11. Jahrhunderts," *Theologische Zeitschrift* (Basel, 1948), p. 2.

44   O. S. Rankin, recently deceased, has published an English translation,

Jewish Religious Polemic of Early and Later Centuries (Edinburgh, 1956), of the debate between Pablo and Nachmanides, an extract from the polemic Niṣṣaḥon of Yomtob Lipmann Mülhausen, and the epistolary dispute between the convert J. H. Rittangel and an Amsterdam Jew over Genesis 49:10, all taken from the Wagenseil edition.

45 This meaningless question must have been very popular at that time. Solomon ibn Verga preserves it for us in a conversation which took place under similar circumstances (Shebeṭ Jehuda 32, fol. 54), in which the Jewish scholar Ephraim ben Sanḥo tells his king (Don Pedro) the fable of the three rings, so that here, mediated through Boccaccio's *Decameron,* we have a prototype of the parable from Lessing's *Nathan.*

46 German translation published by W. Schlessinger, Frankfurt, 1844; English translation published by S. Husik, Philadelphia, 1946, 3 vols.

47 The proof of this point appears as follows: "Whoever considers God as a body or as a power within a body at the same time denies the postulate of God's incorporeal existence." The same passage (I, 13) sees the heresy of Islam as the denial of God's omniscience and providence through the doctrine of fate. Or III, 25: "The Trinity is not to be found in the Pentateuch because this is a doctrine which, upon rational examination, is not compatible with truth; but the law imposes no untrue doctrine upon us, such as that one is equal to three and that the three are one, and yet nevertheless by nature remain distinct, as is asserted."

48 Several replies by Christian theologians prove that the anti-Christian tendency of basing all religious truth upon Albo's three basic doctrines was well understood by the Christian side. For example, we can read about Albo's three dogmas in Johannes Buxtorf the Elder: *Synagoga judaica* (Jüdenschül edition of 1603, pp. 26 f.): "The *unity* of God: hereby he denies the Trinity and the divinity of Christ. *Torah Moshe min ha-shamayim:* hereby he discards the doctrine of Christ and the New Testament, leading to the conclusion that Christ was a false prophet and not the Messiah. *Retribution:* . . . and thereby scorns the passion and death of Christ for the sins of men."

49 From the copious polemic literature, one work deserves to be specially singled out and given the benefit of thorough study: Ḥasdai Crescas' work,

Biṭṭul 'Iḳḳere ha-Noṣrim ("The Refutation of the Basic Christian Dogmas"), which undergirds its arguments with Aristotelian logic.

50 Similarly, *ibid.*, p. 23: "Belief in the Trinity contradicts the first principle, that God is a necessary existence. If we say that the Son is begotten,
then God also is begotten. Now if God is begotten, then he is created and
caused. That is clear, since whatever begets is the cause of his existence. But
whoever is created is not a necessary existence. Thus in this case God would
not be a necessary existence."

51 Cf. D. Neumark: *Geschichte der jüdischen Philosophie des Mittelalters,*
vol. II, part 2, pp. 191 f.

52 On this point, cf. the Breslau dissertation of Stanislaus Simon: *Moses
ben Salomo von Salerno und seiner philosophischen Auseinandersetzungen
mit den Lehren des Christentums nebst erstmaliger Edition des Textes der
"Einwendungen,"* (1931). Moses ben Salomo is neither a very original
thinker, nor is he a unique phenomenon (almost all the Jewish and Arabic
polemic literature against Christianity of the Middle Ages still awaits study
and publication based on the sources!), but the thought processes by which
he counters Trinitarian doctrine, which go deep into scholastic subtleties,
may be considered typical.

53 Now cf. also D. M. Dunlop: *The History of the Jewish Khazars*
(Princeton, 1954), chap 6, pp. 116 ff.

54 I have written about this in "Weiteres zur Auserwählung Israels," *Judaica* 4 (Basel, 1946), now included in the volume *Aus frühchristlicher Zeit.*

55 Referring to Sanhedrin 102a, Rashi emphasizes that no punishment
comes upon Israel in which there is not contained something of punishment
for the sin of the golden calf. Important statements of the Amoraim on this
question are also preserved in the Talmud, 'Aboda Zara 4a.

56 As D. Cassel points out on page 337 of the commentary to his edition of
Kuzari, a parallel train of thought also occurs in Nachmanides (Derashah
p. 5, ed. Jellinek), who himself quotes a passage from Maimonides' Hilḫot
Melaḫim II, 11 (usually censored): "He who considered himself the Messiah

and was condemned to death by the word of the court is foretold in the prophecies of Daniel (11:35) and all suchlike doctrines of the Nazarene and of the Ishmaelite, who arose after him, only serve to prepare the way for the Messiah; the latter will bring the world to perfection, so that all serve God with one will. For the whole world is full of the words which tell of the Messiah, the words of Scripture and the commandments, these words have been disseminated to the farthest coasts, even though in this day some still deny their validity; when the Messiah arises, *they shall all turn back from their errors.*" We should also cite many portions of exegetical and systematic works, e.g., Abrabanel: Preface to the commentary on Isaiah, exegeses of Micah 4:1 ff. and *passim;* David Ḳimḥi on Isa. 2:18, 20; Yalḳut Ḥadash 20, etc.

57 The *Nissaḥon* (Refutation) is of some importance in that (1) it stems from the then completely uneducated circles of German Jewry; (2) in commenting on Christological exegeses, it goes from the defensive to a violent attack upon Christianity; and (3) it reveals a knowledge, remarkable for the Judaism of the day, of the New Testament, as well as the doctrines, customs, and scriptural interpretations of the Church, presumably gained through contact with Christian theologians during the Hussite unrest in Prague. His polemic is often unpleasantly ironical. For example, he replies to an opponent who had taken the plural form in Genesis 1:26: "And God said: 'Let us make man in our image, after our likeness; and let them have dominion over the fish of the sea, and over the fowl of the air, and over the cattle, and over all the earth, and over every creeping thing that creepeth upon the earth.'" ("Let us make men") as a proof of the existence of a Son of God with a sarcastic reference to the singular form in Genesis 1:27 ("And God created man"), saying that the Son had evidently been disobedient and made the Father do the work alone. Such remarks may perhaps be excused on the basis of excessive zeal; but a limit must be set where hair-splitting exegesis reads out of the Scripture whatever is suitable for the immediate attack (e.g., Isa. 5:18, "Woe unto them that draw iniquity with cords of vanity" is referred by Lipmann to the Christian ringing of bells!). It is further of interest that, contrary to most Jewish voices, which refuse expressly to accept responsibility for the death of Jesus, Lipmann states directly that Jesus was executed according to the law concerning blasphemy according to Mishnah Sanhedrin 6, 4, and the decision of the elders can only be praised (ed. Wagenseil, p. 51). The tone of the whole must often be called rudely insulting (e.g., ed. Wagenseil, pp. 15, 40, 42, 56, 80; and *pas-*

sim), the train of logic must be called oversubtle, and one can only agree with C. Siegfried's verdict (Jena address of 1895 on medieval polemic) that there is a lack of "the purer sort of religious perception" in Yomtob Lipmann Mühlhausen. A portion has now been translated into English by O. P. Rankin (cf. note 44).

58   Now cf. also E. L. Dietrich: "Das jüdisch-christliche Religionsgespräch im Ausgang des 16. Jahrhunderts nach dem Handbuch des R. Isaak Troki," *Judaica* XIV (1958), pp. 1-39.

59   These attacks by Troki upon the New Testament once more called Christian apologetics into the field. For example, the orientalist from Greifswald, Brandanus Henricus Gebhardus, as late as 1799 published six Latin disputations of his pupils against the *Ḥizzuḳ 'Emunah*.

60   We follow the very skillful summary of contents by A. Geiger, *Nachgelassene Schriften,* vol. 3, pp. 206 f.

61   On him, cf. Nicéron: *Historie des hommes illustres,* part XI, (Paris, 1739); Abraham van der Hoeven: *De Joh. Clerico et Philippo a Limborch* (Amsterdam, 1843), and its evaluation in H. Ollion—T. J. de Boer: *Lettres inédites de John Locke* (La Haye, 1912), pp. 149-161; and also in C. L. Thysse-Schouten: *Nederlands Cartesianisme* (Leyden, 1954).

62   In view of the many source materials which have so far remained inaccessible, a monograph devoted to him would well repay the labor expended. The Jewish historians Graetz and Kayserling have such monographs planned. Numerous works by Orobio exist only in manuscript, which M. Kayserling lists in *Bibliotheḳa Española-Portugueza-Judaica,* (Strassburg, 1890), pp. 81 ff. There is only one article about him with primarily biographical orientation, that of H. Graetz: "Don Balthasar Isaak Orobio de Castro," MGWJ, 1867. There are further brief references in H. Zöckler: *Der Dialog im Dienste der Apologie, Beweis des Glaubens* (1893), pp. 345 ff. and, by the same man: *Geschichte der Apologie des Christentums* (Gütersloh, 1907), pp. 412 f.; but cf. also note 67.

63   I have discussed Menasseh ben Israel and David de Lara in my article "Schwedisches in der hebräischen Bibliographie," *Nordisk Tidskrift för Bok-*

och Bibliteksväsen (Stockholm, 1946), and the whole period more thoroughly in my book *Philosemitismus im Barock* (Tübingen, 1952).

64 *Praemissis quatuor de Historia Inquisitionis libris* (Amsterdam, 1692), pp. 158, 322 f.; cf. also Le Clerc: *Bibliothèque universelle et historique,* part VII, p. 289. It would be important to initiate inquiry in the trial records in the archives of the Inquisition in Seville.

65 He scourged his contemporaries' tendency toward atheism, resulting from the study of secular knowledge, in his *Epistola invectiva contra Prado, un Philosopho medico,* which exists in many manuscripts. C. Gebhardt (*Uriel da Costa* [Amsterdam, 1922], Introduction pp. xx f.) has reproduced an instructive section of this letter. Now cf. also J. S. Revah: *Spinoza et Juan le Prado,* (Paris, 1959), where this Spanish document is printed for the first time (pp. 86-123).

66 In the ʿEṣ Ḥayyim library of the Portuguese Jewish community in Amsterdam there are further manuscripts of Orobio and Saul Levi Morteiras, which, according to the statement of Jakob Meijer (*Jewish Social Studies* XVIII, 1955, p. 100), should be important for the intellectual climate of the Amsterdam Sephardic community and the history of religious disputations.

67 The work in question is the *Certamen philosophicum* (Amsterdam, 1684), which was directed against Johannes Bredenburg. But he also was in direct correspondence with Spinoza. For Orobio's argument with Spinoza's system, cf. now Joaquin de Carvalho: *Orobio de Castro, e. o. espinosismo* (Coimbra, Portugal, 1938). In 1925, Moses B. Amzalak found in Coimbra another important manuscript by Orobio, and published it: "La Observancia de la Divina Ley de Mosseh."

68 Thus in the preface to da Costa's biography (*Am. Coll.* p. 343) he differentiates expressly a Jew like Orobio from an "atheist" like da Costa, who not only turns against the teachings of Christianity, but also against those of Judaism.

69 These references by Orobio are justified. This is shown by the material which I have assembled on the Jewish thought of the Chiliasts and mystics of the seventeenth century, which I have presented in my book *Philosemitismus im Barock, Religions- und geistesgeschichtliche Untersuchungen* (Tübingen, 1952).

70 For the talmudic doctrine of the twofold form of the Messiah, he refers to the statements of R. Lombrozo in his *Propugnaculum Judaismi,* which was directed against the attacks made by Hugo Grotius in the fifth volume of his work referred to in the next note. This letter, written in Spanish, was never published; it exists only in manuscript.

71 He has in mind the statements of Hugo Grotius in his work *De veritate Religionis christianae* (Leyden, 1622), 1. V, chap. 14-16.

72 The exegesis of Isaiah 53 occupies a central position also in the book *Israel vengée ou exposition naturelle de prophets* (cf. text), which utilizes Orobio's ideas. The first chapter of this work gives a thorough presentation of the difference in rank accorded the law and the prophets according to Jewish doctrine.

73 It should be remarked that *"idolatria"* is used in the Marrano literature as the *terminus technicus* for the Catholic religion. Limborch naturally is indignant over this expression, and points out the idolatry of the people of Israel according to the very accounts of the Torah (p. 278).

74 References may be made to the critical reports in *Bibliothèque Universelle et historique* (1787), part VII, pp. 289-330, and in the *Acta Eruditorum* (Leipzig, 1688), pp. 212-222. Further comparison may be made with the presentation by Zöckler (1893), p. 346.

75 This also struck the attention of John Locke, who saw therein the orthodoxy of Limborch's method of proof vindicated vis-à-vis orthodox criticism (cf. his letter of June 22, 1688, in *Works,* London, 1801, vol. X, p. 17).

76 Cf. L. Zscharnack's edition of John Locke: *Reasonableness of Christianity* (Giessen, 1914), Introduction, p. lii.

77 Locke read the *amica collatio* in manuscript before it was printed, as can be determined from his letters to Limborch of November 24, 1686, and March 31, 1687, edited by Ollion–de Boer, *op. cit.,* pp. 169, 172. In his letter of September 11, 1687 (*Works* X, p. 12), he writes: *"Laudo ego istam tuam erga Judaeum comitatem."*

78   In II, 5 (p. 89), Orobio gives examples of how Jewish apostates became *principes, duces, comites, marchiones, inquisitores, clerici, Canonices, Monachi, et Moniales*—and, in these positions, fierce persecutors of the Jews. Thus, he says (III, 4, p. 102), there are yet today those in Spain who bear highest ecclesiastical dignity whose parents, brothers, and sisters in other lands freely confess to Judaism, who indeed as Jews at the courts of Christian monarchs have already risen to high office. And in the Orient they would rather turn to Islam than be forced further to confess Catholic *idolatria*.

79   Cf. O. Ritschl: *Dogmengeschichte des Protestantismus* III (Göttingen, 1927), pp. 364 ff.; IV (1928), pp. 287 f.

80   For criticism from the orthodox side, cf. *Acta Eruditorum* (April, 1688), pp. 212 ff., and Grousset: *De ternione Controversiarum adv. Judaeos* (Dordrecht, 1688). Further voices can be heard in M. Difenbach: *Judaeus convertendus* (Frankfurt, 1696), pp. 52 f.

81   J. van der Waeyen (*Dissertatio de Logo adv. Joh. Clericum* [Franeker, 1698], p. 175) even charged him with having engaged in the dispute only to give a practical demonstration of the Arminians' principles of toleration.

82   *Morgenröte—Werke* (Gesamtausgabe) IV, 273.

83   Cf. J. W. Petersen: *Nubes testium veritatis de regno Christi* (Frankfurt, 1696), II, p. 119. He says of the division of roles in our dialogue that Orobio gleams with prophetic light because he holds fast to the letter and to the clear promises to the Jewish people, which are still unfulfilled and which may not be misrepresented allegorically.

84   *Die Juden in Portugal* (Leipzig, 1867), p. 304.

85   Cf. the introduction by S. Rawidowicz to the seventh volume of the Akademie edition of Moses Mendelssohn's collected works (Berlin, 1930), which is used for the quotations to follow. In addition, Walter Hoch: "Das Glaubensgespräch zwischen J. C. Lavater und M. Mendelssohn," *Judaica* 1947, 1-2; L. Baeck: *Von Moses Mendelssohn zu Franz Rosenzweig* (Stuttgart, 1958).

86 Cf. H. J. Schoeps: *Geschichte der jüdischen Religionsphilosophie in der Neuzeit* (Berlin, 1935), vol. I, pp. 14 ff.

87 Even among the rabbis contemporary with Mendelssohn—the last real ghetto generation in Germany—there is no basically different view, although the *moral* viewpoint characteristic of the age controls the verdict and leads to far-reaching toleration. Thus we read in a letter, "Seder Olam," written in the year 1757, by R. Jacob Emden (Altona), who was also in correspondence with Mendelssohn, as follows: "The founder of Christianity did the heathen a great good deed by removing idolatry from them, subjecting them to the seven Noachite laws, and thus giving them a *moral doctrine!*"

88 Collected works, vol. II, pp. 321 f.: "Among all the prescriptions and precepts of the Mosaic law there is not a single one which says, Thou shalt believe; but rather they all say, Thou shalt do." And in a letter to Elkan Herz of July 23, 1771, we read: "We have no doctrines of faith which go against reason or go beyond it. We add nothing more to natural religion than commandments, ordinances, and precepts, but the basic principles of belief of our religion rest upon the foundation of reason; they are in agreement with the results of study in all areas without any contradiction or conflict."

89 For this reason he must decline Lavater's missionary attempt, which hoped to effect the conversion of all others with that of Mendelssohn. Mendelssohn adds an additional weighty argument by alluding to Pauline theology: "It is incomprehensible why the Nazarenes wish to convert us, thus destroying the visible proof of their faith." (III, pp. 105 f.)

90 In *Geschichte der jüd. Religionsphilosophie* I, pp. 24 f., I have enlarged upon the way in which, in the case of the "third Moses," the free, unfathomable, and undefinable God of revelation was transformed into the intellectually necessary God of the highest good and most perfect reason, how thus the *prima causa* usurps the place of *creatio ex nihilo,* the avenging righteousness of God is reduced to punishment based on wise kindness, wonder become passive, the expectation of a personal Messiah vanishes, only the giving of the law is left of the phenomenon of revelation, and therefore—as Steinheim ironically said—it would only be *sensible* "to send his laws after the ejected God."

91 Here, out of honest conviction, Mendelssohn follows the traditional line, discarding the game of Christological interpretation contrary to the sense of the words with the following statement: "I think I understand the language of the text as well as any innovator, for it is my second mother tongue. It seems to me that these passages contain not the least trace of a proof. The interpretations of the passages made by the theologians have appeared to me in many passages to be plainly wrong, and, in the rest, extremely forced and arbitrary." (VII, p. 302)

92 He writes to Bonnet about the Christian Unitarians: "I must confess to you honestly that this religious party seems to me to belong more to Judaism than to the really dominant Christian religion. From whatever side I view this doctrine, it agrees much more with the essential articles of the Jewish faith than with the basic truths of the Christian faith." (III, pp. 105 f.) Of course, he admits that the expectation of a messianic national king would still separate the Jews even from the Unitarians.

93 It is well known that this letter received an answer from Schleiermacher, as well as from Propst Teller *et al.;* all in all, it occasioned twenty-three independent rebuttals (cf. Ellen Littmann's study of the repercussions in ZGJD 1936, 2-3). It is a valuable document for the spiritual condition of the educated Jews of Berlin at the turn of the century, who wanted to free themselves of the chains of the ceremonial law, and were so "enlightened" that they only suggested, as a condition for their conversion, that the Christian side revise its irrational dogmas. That these suggestions could seriously be debated proves only that blindness to religious values has hardly ever gone further.

94 Cf. also Hermann Cohen: *Jüdische Schriften* (Berlin, 1924), vol. I, pp. 284 ff. For Kant, Judaism was essentially an "embodiment of merely statutory laws," which contradict "purely ethical precepts," a kind of national constitution of the Jewish national community, and thus actually "not a religion at all" (Kant's *Gesammelte Shriften,* ed. Hartenstein, VI, 24). This seemed all too well confirmed by Mendelssohn's theory of religion. Nevertheless, with his primacy of the practical reason, he provided points of contact with Jewish religious teaching, because he fixed the postulate of freedom, made room for faith beyond the limits of reason, and—what seemed especially significant to Steinheim—recognized the Mosaic doctrine of

creation and affirmed it as philosophically relevant (*Kr. d. pr. Vernuft*). All this has again and again given Kant an important place in the basic philosophical work of Jewish theology. In this context, it may be considered of interest that Hegel saw the principles of "Mosaism" and Kantian "legal morality" as *one* (in each case the second phase of development).

95   For Hegel's verdict on Judaism, cf. *Vorlesungen über die Philosophie der Geschichte,* ed. Lasson, vol. II, pp. 457 f.; *Grundlehre der Philosophie des Rechts,* ed. Lasson, sec. 278 and 338; *Phänomenologie des Geistes,* sec. 484 and elsewhere. For the preservation of the Hegelian view among his "orthodox" pupils in Protestant theology, cf. Ph. Marheinecke: *Grundlinien der christlichen Dogmatik,* sec. 335 and 276. More specific data now in H. J. Schoeps: "Die ausserchristlichen Religionen bei Hegel," ZRGG VII (1955), pp. 28 ff.

96   This was done for the first time by Schoeps: *Geschichte etc.,* chap. 4 and 5. For Formstecher, cf. now also B. Bamberger: "Formstecher's History of Judaism," HUCA 23, 2 (1950).

97   And this, because as a strict Hegelian, Hirsch saw his task solely to be the demonstration that Judaism was "the absolute religion," while Formstecher at least makes an effort to adjust his system, however distantly, to the course of history. In Hirsch's constructions of the religious history of mankind, Christianity appears more as a kind of transitory false doctrine which nevertheless will have the net result (thanks to the "cunning of the idea") of bringing Gentile mankind to God via this detour. His chain of thought, philosophically more significant than Formstecher's, resembles the latter in many points; only, in the case of each of them, the absolute nature of Judaism does not occupy a dogmatic position of historical truth in the traditional sense, but appears as a dogmatic necessity of conceptual philosophic speculation. As a result of the involved nature of their systems, Formstecher and Hirsch no more engaged in dialogue than did their great examples, Schelling and Hegel.

98   *Ibid.,* 450: "It may not hurl itself into paganism in order to assimilate paganism organically to itself, because it must always assert itself as representative of attained subjectivity."

99 Formstecher studied all the material on the history of religion collected by Schelling and Hegel; for his own purposes, and partially with a change of evaluation, he worked them into his special construction of the history of religion. In addition, it should be emphasized here that Formstecher was, in general, a well-educated man of widest reading, who absolutely kept pace with the scholarship of his day. For example, he is acquainted with the most important dogmatic and exegetical literature of evangelical theology of his generation. Frequent quotations are taken from Nietzsche, Bretschneider, Marheinecke, De Wette, Neander, *et al.*

100 Of course, such thoughts lay ready to hand in the age which gave birth to them. The Jewish liberalism of the nineteenth century had a much more vague and unclear belief in any missionary task of Judaism, even though it spoke of a "transitory representative of the religion of the spirit," preferring to glorify the exemplary character of Jewish ethics, and declaring the eventual acceptance of these ethics by all members of educated mankind as the goal of the Messianic Age.

101 *Vom Bleibenden und Vergänglichen im Judentum,* ed. Schoeps (Berlin, 1935), p. 48. Steinheim anticipated the results of much later study in the history of religion in the conversation, here published, with August Twestan, Schleiermacher's successor in Berlin, and his young friend. For example, a very similar summary is given by H. Gunkel: *Zum religionsgeschichtlichen Verständnis des Neuen Testaments* (1903), p. 35: "Early Christianity is like a river in which two other great rivers have flowed together: the one is specifically Israelitic, derived from the Old Testament; but the other flows from alien Oriental religions." In his *Dogmengechichte,* I, 1, as is well known, Harnack described the history of the development of dogma in early Christianity as the mixture of Jewish religious material with other material from the ancient Near East, as well as Hellenistic philosophy by way of so-called gnosis.

102 We might refer in this connection to the conversations at the beginning of this century between the last of the great cabalists of Western Europe, Elie Benamozegh (Livorno), and the young French Catholic Aimée Pallière. These ended with Pallière becoming a "Noachite" and the spokesman of liberal Judaism in France. For Pallière, cf. Marion Nordmann-Schwarze: *Aimée Pallière, das Leben eines Noachiden,* in *Lebendiger Geist,*

a collection of essays in honor of H. J. Schoeps, ed. H. Diwald (Leyden, 1959), pp. 75 ff.

103 Reprinted as an appendix to Franz Rosenzweig: *Briefe* (Berlin, 1935). Fully aware of what the statement means, I should like to say that these letters constitute one of the most important publishing events of the twentieth century, both for the intellectual history and the theology of the immediate past. Data on Franz Rosenzweig can be obtained from a monograph by N. N. Glatzer: *Franz Rosenzweig, His Life and Thought* (New York, 1953).

104 Hereby, Rosenzweig also renewed the ancient Jewish protest against Christian reinterpretation of Scripture, particularly against typological interpretation. Cf. p. 707: "The Old Testament has ceased to be a collection of 'types' (the people of God as the type of the Church), and it *will* cease to be a collection of prophecies, the more the prophecies are shown to be fulfilled." Many important perceptions and remarks on biblical hermeneutics are contained in the work by Buber-Rosenzweig: *Die Schrift und ihre Verdeutschung* (Berlin, 1936). Their translation of the Bible gives positive evidence of a new (*sc.* scriptural) attitude toward the words of the Bible; in spite of many reservations toward the etymological procedure, the work can be given the status of a modern German "Targum."

105 Rosenzweig clearly means in the Midrash! I have treated the theme in more detail in "The Sacrifice of Isaac in Paul's Theology," *JBL* 1946, which is found on pp. 144-152 of the German edition of my work on Paul.

106 The positive trend of this idea reveals a special missionary task of Israel. Cf. the continuation of the thought fifteen years later in the ambitious sociological history of Eugen Rosenstock-Huessy: *Europäische Revolutionen* (Jena, 1931), pp. 376 f; 3rd edition (Stuttgart, 1960) pp. 383 f.

107 The verbatim account of the dialogue according to the stenographic record was published in the *Theologische Blätter* of September, 1933. Buber's answer, amplified, was printed in the volume *Die Stunde und die Erkenntnis* (Berlin, 1936).

108 This lecture was published in the collection *Kampf um Israel* (Berlin, 1933).

109   The parallel passage from the 1930 lecture, "Die Brennpunkte der jüdischen Seele" (in *Kampf um Israel,* p. 65), runs as follows: "That which ultimately differentiates between Judaism and Christianity is the non-incarnational nature of the God who reveals himself to flesh and encounters flesh in mutual relationship, as well as the lack of a caesura in human history, which is aimed at fulfillment and forever experiences decision."

110   Once again, the parallel passage from the earlier lecture (*ibid.,* p. 53): "The primary word which has been spoken by God in regard to this possibility of his being recognized again is his statement to Moses from the burning bush: 'I shall be present as him, as whom I shall be present.' He is always there, he is always present to his creatures, but each time as him, as whom he is present here and now, so that the mind of man is not able to know in advance the clothing of existence and situation in which God will show himself at any time. The important thing is to recognize him once again, in whatever form he may be clothed."

111   Cf. now also Franz Frh. v. Hammerstein: *Das Messiasrproblem bei Martin Buber* (Stuttgart, 1958), and G. Lindeskrog: "Das Problem des Glaubens in der Exegese M. Bubers," SEÅ 1957, pp. 218-239.

112   Cf. Romano Guardini: *Das Bild van Jesus dem Christus im Neuen Testament* (Würzburg, 1936): "It is the living, divine-human existence of Jesus Christ which awakens faith—not faith which engenders his divine-human nature. Only a faith based on reality has the power to overcome the world, such as belonged and still belongs to the Christian conviction." (Pp. 32)

113   The meaning which the Old Testament must have for the Church of Christ must be examined objectively from a theological point of view. This question ultimately concerns the very existence of Christianity in the world today. The essential point threatens to be surrendered if the Old Testament and its law—with and in spite of its peculiar Jewish character—is not held fast as a piece of Judaism continuing to live on in Christianity, in spite of all pagan temptations. The entire question is one of *proper* theological recognition and justification of this fact. The discussion within Protestantism has not yet been able to find this. For example, what is one to make of it when even the most recent study of the Old Testament—under the inspiration of

dialectic theology—results in such fantastic trains of thought as are to be found in the periodical *Evangelische Theologie* (1936, 9): "Israel, too, has a presence of Christ . . . in that Christ himself is present to the ancient nation in the witness of Scripture. The reasoning is as follows: *in* the words of Scripture (*sc.* the Old Testament) as the words of faith-righteousness, Christ is *present* as him who speaks these words. The words of Scripture not only *point to him,* but *come from him;* and therein he is *present in the Scriptures* as the Christ." This reduction of history to a single principle in the style of Hengstenberg (not at all necessary *ad maiorem Christi gloriam*) is not more justified by the phenomena than is the other possibility of radical dualism, which the Christian faith could probably bear even less. For example, R. Bultmann is treading on very thin ice when he takes a genuine insight and exaggerates it in the opposite direction (*Glaube und Verstehen,* pp. 333 f.): "The events which said something for Israel, were God's word—for us they have nothing more to say. . . . Israel's history is not revelatory history for the Christian faith. . . . Insofar as God has acted graciously in that history, that history has no value for us." Precisely because of its simplification of the problem (from our point of view, coming nearer to proper exegesis), such a theology is in danger of cutting its own umbilical cord, which binds together Christianity and the Old Testament, including that portion of the law which, through the transformation of Pauline doctrine, has become law for the nations of the earth. Whoever wants to go beyond Paul can only end up with Marcion!

114   The reasoning is given in more detail in my *Paulus,* chap. V.

115   Cf. now the last chapter of my book *Was ist der Mensch? Philosophische Anthropologie als Einführung in die Geistesgeschichte der neuesten Zeit* (Göttingen, 1960).

116   Cf. also what I have said in my book on Paul about the "shared expectation that the decisive event is yet to come—as the goal of the ways of God, along which HE goes with mankind in Israel and in the Church. The Church of Jesus Christ has preserved no representation of its Lord and Saviour. If Jesus were to return tomorrow, no Christian would recognize him by his face. But it could well be that he who comes at the end of time, who is the expectation of the Synagogue as well as of the Church, has the *same* countenance." (P. 274)

ABBREVIATIONS

HUCA	Hebrew Union College Annula, Cincinnati
JBL	Journal of Biblical Literature, Philadelphia
JE	Jüdische Enzyklopädie, Berlin
JQR	Jewish Quarterly Review, Philadelphia
MGWJ	Monatsschrift für Geschichte und Wissenschaft des Judentums
MPG	J. P. Migne: *Patrologiae cursus completus, series graeca.*
MPL	————. *Patrologiae cursus completus, series latina.*
SEÅ	Svensk Exegetisk Årsbok, Uppsala
ThBl	Theologische Blätter
ZGJD	Zeitschrift für Geschichte der Juden in Deutschland, Berlin
ZRGG	Zeitschrift für Religions—und Geistesgeschichte, Leyden—Cologne

ENGLISH EDITIONS OF WORKS MENTIONED IN TEXTS AND NOTES

Bloch, J. S. *Israel and the Nations* (Berlin-Vienna, 1927).

Buber, Martin. *Kampf um Israel.* In *Mamre,* essays in religion by Martin Buber (Melbourne & London, 1946).

Eisenmenger. *Entdecktes Judentum.* In *Rabbinical Literature,* trans. Rev. J. P. Stehelin (London, 1748).

Grotius, Hugo. *De Veritate Religionis Christianae. The Truth of the Christian Religion* (London, 1805).

Harnack, Adolf. *Dogmengeschichte. History of Dogma* (New York, 1958).

Hegel, Georg. *Philosophie der Religion. Lectures on the Philosophy of Religion* (New York, n.d.).

————. *Vorlesungen über die Philosophie der Geschichte. Lectures on the Philosophy of History* (New York, 1956).

————. *Grundlehre der Philosophie des Rechts. Hegel's Philosophy of Right* (Oxford, 1942).

————. *Phänomenologie des Geistes. The Phenomenology of Mind* (New York, 1931).

Judah ha-Levi. *Kuzari. Kitab al Khazari* (New York, 1927).

Justin Martyr, St. *Dialogue with Trypho* (London, 1930).

Klausner, Joseph. *Jesus von Nazareth. Jesus of Nazareth* (New York, 1925).

Lavater, Johann Caspar. *Physiognomische Fragmente. Essays on Physiognomy* (London, 1860).

Lessing, Gotthold Ephraim. *Nathan der Weise. Nathan the Wise* (New York, 1917).

Locke, John. *Lettres inédites de John Locke.* cf. *The Works of John Locke* (London, 1824).

Origen. *Contra Celsum. Against Celsus,* trans. H. Chadwick (Cambridge, 1953).

Orobio de Castro, Isaac. *Israel vengée ou exposition naturelle de prophetes. Israel Defended* (London, 1938).

Rosenstock-Huessy, Eugen. *Europäische Revolutionen. Out of Revolution: Autobiography of Western Man* (New York, 1938).

Schoeps, H. J. *Paulus. Paul* (Philadelphia, 1961).

Troki, Isaac ben Abraham. *Ḥizzuḳ 'Emunah. Hizzuk Emunah,* or *Faith Strengthened* (London, 1851).

Since 1945, the following significant contributions to the theme of this book have been published:

Blumenkranz, Bernhard. *Die Judenpredigt Augustins, ein Beitrag zur Geschichte der jüdisch-christlichen Beziehungen in den ersten Jahrhunderten* (Basel, 1946).

———. *Juifs et Chrétiens dans le monde oriental (430-1096)* (Paris, 1960).

Brandon, S. G. F. *The Fall of Jerusalem in the Christian Church* (London, 1951).

Daube, David. *The New Testament and Rabbinic Judaism* (London, 1956).

Davies, W. D. *Paul and Rabbinic Judaism* (London, 1949).

Dix, Gregory. *Jew and Greek in the Primitive Church* (London, 1953).

Goppelt, Leonhard. *Christentum und Judentum im ersten und zweiten Jahrhundert* (Gütersloh, 1954).

Hasler, V. E. *Gesetz und Evangelium in der alten Kirche bis Origenes* (Zürich, 1958).

Hendenquist, Göte (ed.). *The Church and the Jewish People* (Edinburgh, 1954).

Isaac, Jules. *Jesus et Israel* (Paris, 1959).

Jocz, Jacob. *The Jewish People and Jesus Christ* (London, 1949).

Maurer, Wilhelm. *Kirche und Synagoge, Motive und Formen der Ausein-*

andersetzung der Kirche mit dem Judentum im Laufe der Geschichte (Stuttgart, 1953).

Oepke, Albert. *Das neue Gottesvolk* (Gütersloh, 1950).

Parkes, James G. *Judaism and Christianity* (London, 1948).

————. *The Foundations of Judaism and Christianity* (London, 1960).

Rankin, O. S. *Jewish Religious Polemic of Early and Later Centuries* (Edinburgh, 1956).

Schoeps, Hans Joachim. *Theologie und Geschichte des Judenchristentums* (Tübingen, 1949).

————. *Aus frühchristlicher Zeit / Religionsgeschichtliche Untersuchungen* (Tübingen, 1950).

————. *Philosemitismus im Barock* (Tübingen, 1952).

————. *Paulus—die Theologie des Apostels im Lichte der jüdischen Religionsgeschichte* (Tübingen, 1959).

————. *Grundlehren des jüdischen Glaubens, Textbuch zur deutschen systematischen Theologie* (Stuttgart, 1961).

Shalom ben Chorin. *Die Antwort des Jona* (Hamburg, 1953).

Simon, Marcel. *Verus Israel. Étude sur les Relations entre Chrétiens et Juifs dans l'Empire Romain (135-425)* (Paris, 1948).

Thieme, Karl. *Kirche und Synagoge, die ersten nachbiblischen Zeugnisse ihres Gegensatzes im Offenbarungsverständnis* (Olten, 1945).

Wilde, Robert. *The Treatment of the Jews in the Greek Christian Writers of the First Three Centuries* (Washington, 1945).

INDEX